DISMANTLING
THE STATE

DISMANTLING THE STATE

The Theory and Practice of Privatization

By
Dr Madsen Pirie

First published in 1985 by
The National Center for Policy Analysis
©Dr Madsen Pirie

The views expressed in this publication are those of the author and do not necessarily reflect those of the publisher. This book is published as a contribution to public debate.

ISBN 0-906517-58-3

Printed in the United States

CONTENTS

Page

FOREWORD   vii
  By Dr John Goodman

1. INTRODUCTION   1

2. THE PERFORMANCE OF THE PUBLIC SECTOR   6

3. THE ATTEMPTS TO OVERCOME PUBLIC
   SECTOR PROBLEMS   17

4. DISMANTLING THE STATE   24

5. THE TECHNIQUES   30

6. FUTURE PRIVATIZATION IN BRITAIN   109

7. CONCLUSION   113

'In every great monarchy of Europe the sale of the crown lands would produce a very large sum of money, which, if applied to the payment of the public debts, would deliver from mortgage a much greater revenue than any which those lands have ever afforded to the crown... When the crown lands had become private property, they would, in the course of a few years, become well-improved and well cultivated.'

Adam Smith, *The Wealth of Nations*,
Book V Chapter II, Part I.

FOREWORD

Once in a rare while a book is written which is destined to have impact and cause change. That such books are rare is evidenced by the fact that fundamental change in the direction of social events is rare. Yet, Dr Madsen Pirie, President of the Adam Smith Institute in London, has written such a book.

This is a book about ideas — ideas that cause change. Although its context is contemporary British politics, its message transcends political boundaries and cultural institutions. Although the focus of the analysis is the great privatization experiment being directed by Margaret Thatcher, in many ways this is a book about political change as such.

There are two types of ideas that cause change. The distinction hinges on who benefits from an idea's creation. Some ideas benefit chiefly the individuals who originate them. Other ideas benefit chiefly society as a whole. Both types of ideas can be found in the marketplace as well as in the political sector.

Ideas which benefit mainly their creators are part of a natural and spontaneous order. This is an order which arises from the voluntary interaction of individuals exercising freedom of choice in the pursuit of self-interest. In this respect, ideas that work are similar to products that work. An individual who sees a way to reduce production costs or to make a product more valuable to consumers might seize the idea, refine it, and implement it to his own advantage. In this case, the reward for discovering an idea that works is increased profit.

Ideas which benefit mainly others are not part of the natural order. Since the originators of these ideas cannot appropriate their value, incentives to create these ideas are weak, despite the fact that their overall value may be enormous. Because there is no natural incentive system which induces the creation of ideas that are of great value to society as a whole, progressive societies quite properly attempt to honor in other ways the individuals who originate them.

Important political and social changes are almost always the product of both types of ideas. Fundamental change requires that the individuals who seek and discover ways of promoting change find it profitable to do so. Yet, fundamental change also requires intellectual advocacy: a systematic explanation of what the change is all about and why it is good, and a general defense of the change against proposed alternatives. It is this talent for building the general case for change that is rare and difficult to come by.

An example of how both types of ideas combine to create fundamental change is illustrated by the capitalist revolution of the late eighteenth and early nineteenth centuries. When Adam Smith wrote *The Wealth of Nations* he was not discovering the benefits of capitalism. Those benefits already had been discovered by the people who traded daily in the marketplace. In other words, they already knew how they benefited individually from freedom of trade.

The accomplishment of *The Wealth of Nations* was to provide a general case for capitalism — an intellectual explanation and a moral defense of a process that already was well underway. Adam Smith focused on the general benefits of capitalism to society as a whole, rather than on the specific benefits to individuals. In doing so, he helped sustain and rejuvenate a movement that otherwise might have died.

Madsen Pirie has accomplished a similar synthesis of theory and practice. He suspects, as do I, that we are standing on the threshold of a revolution. It is a revolution which is not confined to any one country, but is worldwide in scope and effect. It is a revolution which is comparable to the revolution of capitalism in the last century and the revolution of communism in this one. To my knowledge, Pirie is the first to have grasped the nature of this revolution, to have described how it works and why it promises to great benefits for us all.

Privatization is the process of transferring activities from the public sector to the private sector. In Britain, such transfers are taking place on a massive scale. A primary reason for the success of privatization is that it arises naturally from the spontaneous, unplanned decisions of thousands of disparate individuals. There are many barriers to privatization erected by opponents of change. Yet, these barriers are being surmounted daily by people who find it in their economic self-interest to do so. One reason why privatization is working in Britain is that people are finding it in their self-interest to dismantle the state.

Yet such a process cannot be sustained and continued without a general intellectual case to guide, promote and defend it. That is the accomplishment of this book. It is a book to be read and re-read by all who would seek to live in a new order, based on individual freedom and individual choice.

John C. Goodman
President
National Center for Policy Analysis

1. INTRODUCTION

Although the term 'free enterprise' is conventionally used to describe the economic systems of the United States and Britain the salient characteristic of both economies is the size of the public sector. In the United states, as in Britain, the government is the largest single element in the system. It is the biggest consumer, the biggest employer, and far and away the biggest spender. Besides being the largest element of both economies, government also exerts a distorting effect on such freedom of action as survives in the private sector.

In the free enterprise portion of the economy, people express themselves through personal decisions. They reveal their priorities with spending decisions. They seize entrepreneurial opportunities. They take chances, and run the risk of winning or losing. The public sector prevents these activities. Instead it responds to political, rather than economic, pressures. It pre-empts the funds which citizens would have used to make their own choices. It spends for the benefit of special interest groups funds which could have sustained entrepreneurial activity.

Although people talk of the public sector as though it expresses choices made by the public, it in fact expresses the priorities of legislators and bureaucrats. The property and capital which are called public are administered by these individuals as if it were their own. Ultimately, this means that the public sector takes resources out of the area in which the beneficial disciplines of the market operate. It takes them away from the trial and error activities, and from the choices by which people introduce their preferences into the system. It removes resources from the progressive and growth-generating sector, and locks them into programs which satisfy political constituencies.

If a dispassionate observer looked at the history of the United States and Britain, he or she might conclude that the gradual growth of the public sector was part of the life cycle of a free enterprise economy. Looking at the steady and remorseless increase in the proportion of the economy falling under the government's grip, the observer might well suppose this trend to be inevitable, and one which would culminate in the extinction of the remaining free enterprise activities.

Commentators have already noted a 'ratchet effect' which sustains the public sector. Like an industrial cog-wheel which can turn in one direction only, the size of government increases but never diminishes. Free-spending administrations can always increase the scope and extent of their activities, but more cautious legislators are unable to decrease them in times of stringency. The political system makes it very easy for Congress to vote for increased spending, or to legislate automatic increases in spending. That same system makes it almost impossible to cut spending. New projects can be taken on without difficulty, but older ones cannot be jettisoned.

The cumulative effect over the decades has been to increase the size of the public sector year by year until it now limits the spontaneous society — the realm of private decision making — to a small part of the whole. A regimented and regulated society now forms the dominant element and many speculate on how long the growth of the public sector can continue before it so restricts the market sector that it completely absorbs it.

From time to time administrations have been elected amid much rhetoric about cutting public spending. None of them has succeeded in doing so. At best there has been no more than a temporary holding action, perhaps only a slowing down of the rate of increase. Although political mythology has it that these politicians were not tough enough, the evidence suggests they were simply unable to fulfill their brave words. Intentions alone are insufficient to curtail public spending.

Given the history of these attempts, the prognosis for free societies cannot be described as optimistic. These societies seem to face the prospect of ever-greater burdens on the productive sector to support an ever-increasing number of beneficiaries of state largesse. Industry, saddled with the additional costs of government, seems destined to produce goods and services more and more expensively. The outlook is for a constant and increasing export of jobs to developing countries whose lower costs promise to help them capture the markets of the advanced economies.

This, in turn, raises the specter of protectionism. A wall around America and other developed countries might allow them to produce and sell expensive goods to their own captive markets by keeping out the competition. Unfortunately, this promises an international grouping of independent fortress economies, all stagnating under high costs. The simultaneous eclipse of economic freedom and economic prosperity is not an attractive combination to look forward to, but to many there seems no other way to relieve the legislature from the mounting pressures to sustain and increase the growth of the public sector.

A new approach

It is onto this landscape that the word *'privatization'* is making its appearance on the political horizon. Privatization, as pioneered by the Thatcher government in Britain, involves transferring the production of goods and services from the public sector to the private sector. At its lowest common denominator, it means having the private sector accomplish that which was previously done by the public sector.

Close to the heart of the case for privatization lies the recognition that private programs are subject to economic disciplines, and respond to choices made by the beneficiaries of these programs. While it might be impossible to control the cost and scope of a public program, if such a program can be moved to the private sector it automatically becomes subject to market-based disciplines.

In effect, privatization controls the public sector by dismantling it. Thus, it offers a 'reverse ratchet', a means of systematically reducing the public, government-directed part of the economy. Once a program is operating successfully outside of the state sector, it can stay there. Each piece of privatization can thus permanently diminish the overall scope of state involvement in the economy.

Privatization is not something peculiar to the British economy. Although the trail was blazed there, and perhaps was most needed there, its fire is spreading rapidly. West Germany,

Belgium and other European economies are witnessing its inroads. In the Pacific, it is beginning to dominate Japanese thinking. Malaysia, Singapore, and Taiwan already have major privatization projects under way; and even Communist countries including Vietnam and the People's Republic of China have been affected by its progress.

Part of the universal appeal of privatization lies in the fact that it is not a policy but an *approach*. It is an approach which recognizes that the regulation which the market imposes on economic activity is superior to any regulation which men can devise and operate by law. It is an approach which also recognizes that the market measures, and responds to, the choices and preferences of people more accurately than the political process. A program performed in the private economy can be done more efficiently, more cheaply, and with greater satisfaction to its beneficiaries than its counterpart can achieve in the public sector.

It is quite wrong to suppose that privatization is solely a policy for getting rid of nationalized industries. It is also wrong to suppose that America, which has few nationalized industries, has little to gain by it. Privatization is a process by which the public sector is reduced by transferring its functions to the private sector.

Public spending in the United States, which shows no sign of being susceptible to other restraints, could be brought under control by the use of privatization. It has a part to play in releasing into the private economy assets controlled by government at the federal, state and local levels. Industries which are owned and operated by government at all levels are potential candidates, and many, even most, of the services provided by government could be performed in the private sector. Privatization, as an approach, also could make inroads into the regulatory functions of government, and into the system of transfer payments and entitlement programs.

A program of privatization in the United States would have a contribution to make in areas such as federal lands, Amtrak, public housing, social security, education, regulation of industry and energy, and even food stamps. Any program which legislators have been unable to control by other means is a candidate for private sector operation.

While privatization is not a policy, it still less is an easy formula. It requires creativity to devise policies appropriate to each public sector problem. Solutions which have been successful in one country often will not succeed in another. Even within a country, policies which successfully deal with one problem cannot necessarily be applied to another.

Experience has shown that not only is each country different, but each problem is different. The process of privatization requires policies to be tailor-made to deal with each particular issue. Each part of the public sector generates different interest groups and different political problems. Each distinct program requires a distinct approach.

However, the experience of other countries, including Britain, is relevant for the United States because it shows the various approaches in action and the results which can be achieved. What it does not necessarily show are the specific policies needed to solve the problems of America's public sector. Because America's problems are different, so will be many of the solutions.

Nonetheless, the British experience shows what can be done. It illustrates the battery of privatization techniques which have been developed and applied already. It serves, above all, as an incentive to policy analysts to devise creative solutions which are relevant to the US scene. If they respond to that challenge, then privatization offers the first real chance to reverse the growth of government and restore to individuals the freedom and the choices which government has usurped.

2. THE PERFORMANCE OF THE PUBLIC SECTOR

Attitudes toward the public sector of the economy often have colored the way its performance has been evaluated. While the private production of goods and services has been assessed in terms of normal commercial criteria (profitability, efficiency, consumer satisfaction, etc.), state activity has been viewed as a public service which is different in kind and which requires a different standard of judgement.

As a result of this double standard, private undertakings have been judged by comparing their performance with that of their rivals. Public activities on the other hand, have been judged against what was intended. In socialist economies this reaches its ultimate point when economic performance is assessed in terms of whether the targets of a five year plan have been attained. Even in mixed economies, there has been a strong tendency to judge the success or failure of public undertakings against some concept of what 'ought' to have been achieved.

A central assumption has been that public sector operations cannot be judged by normal economic criteria. On the contrary, it has been widely supposed that government activities, requiring no profits to provide a return to shareholders, operate in a league whose performance is assessed by non-economic factors. Thus, the quality of service is often gauged against what can 'reasonably be expected' from the labor force, or from the available funding.

A parallel but less explicit assumption has been that readiness to serve the public provides a motivation in public sector employees that is equally as strong as the profit motive in the private economy. This assumption has been particularly prevalent in the areas of public activity which involve regulation and administration, as opposed to the production of goods and services.

The measurement of performance against expectations, and the assumption of a selfless workforce, have provided a formidable combination against objective assessment of the public sector. These assumptions have worked to insulate the public sector from comparisons of cost-effectiveness and quality of service. Had the public economy been treated as simply another way of organizing the production of goods and services, it might have been evaluated dispassionately against its alternatives. Had there been no assumption of selfless public service, ways might have been developed to link the aims of the producers with the satisfaction of public needs.

Recent analysis

Only recently have analysts stood aside from these assumptions and produced studies which evaluate public performance by more conventional and realistic standards. The comparative efficiency of production and delivery of public goods and services has been judged in two ways. First, the use of foreign examples has enabled assessments to be made even in cases of national monopoly. Although largely invulnerable to any unfavourable contrasts within a country, a national monopoly can be compared with the performance of its private counterparts in other countries. The quantity and quality of service which is achieved for each given input can be measured, as can less obvious criteria including the extent of technological improvements and the variety of services offered to the consumers.

The second type of comparison which recently has been employed is comparison with private sector counterparts within a country. Even in cases of local or national monopoly, there are often comparable private sector activities with which to compare performance. In fields as diverse as transportation and housing, education and health, there are private sources of production that enable comparisons of cost and productivity. Even in areas such as transfer payments and regulation, there are equivalents lying outside of the public sector which can be used for critical comparison.

Once we overcome the assumption that the public sector is different in kind and that it is entitled to a different standard of evaluation, these alternative assessments become admissible.

To some extent it is the visibly poor performance of the public sector which has contributed to the abandonment of those benign, but faulty assumptions. It is the result of hard-nosed, more realistic comparisons which have transformed the intellectual perception of the public sector.

In place of the image of a beneficial and helpful arm of society, the public sector is now largely perceived as afflicted by a number of serious economic and institutional problems. A systematic examination of these problems leads to a new picture of the public sector, and a new recognition of its limitations.

TEN PROBLEM AREAS

There are ten basic problem areas which emerge from an examination of the public sector. These problem areas merit close inspection because when taken together they cast doubt on the use of public sector organization to produce and deliver goods and services. These problems are not simply adverse tendencies which need to be monitored and corrected. They are structural weaknesses which undermine the whole basis on which the public sector is established.

1. Production costs

Several major studies have compared the costs of producing the same goods and services in both the private and public sectors. All have concluded that the public sector costs are much higher. The margin of savings achieved by the private sector varies with the type of good or service being produced. It also varies from country to country. Despite these variations, comparative studies all point in the same direction and identify a range of cost savings to be expected where private enterprise is used. On average, private industry in Britain has costs of production that are about 33 percent lower than in the public sector. In the United States the figure is nearer to 40 percent and in West Germany, private business produces goods and services at 50 percent of the cost of production by its public counterpart.

It is important to compare like with like. The costs of public sector operations are often very difficult to calculate because of the difficulty in distributing overhead expenses. A valid comparison must count the cost of central administration, of buildings and insurance, of recruitment and training, and of fringe benefits. Even more important, it must count the cost of capital. These calculations, long routine in private business, are by no means the norm in public activity.

The strikingly lower cost of the private alternative emerges in study after study where like-with-like comparisons are drawn. It appears that market-induced pressures to keep costs down and profits up act as a better discipline on the private sector than does the desire for economy in the public sector. Private businesses seem able to achieve cost-cutting and productivity gains which the public sector cannot match.

2. Efficiency

The comparisons made for similar types of operations all point to greater efficiency as the source of private business's lower costs. The studies indicate that public operations tend to use higher manpower levels for identical operations, and make much less efficient use of their machines.

Typical are the studies on garbage collection. The private operators were found to use fewer employees per vehicle, and to have the vehicles in active use for a greater number of hours each week. Single-man or two-man operations were the norm in the private sector, whereas the public operations frequently featured five-man operations. Turn-around time for vehicle repair was faster for private businesses, and the time spent on the road was greater.

The implication, once again, seems to be that the disciplines of competition and the need to earn a profit keep private businesses leaner and more efficient than their public counterparts. A private firm can go bankrupt if it fails to keep up with the competition; public sector activities rarely face a similar prospect. The different penalties which they face seem to produce a difference in performance.

3. Labor costs

Labor costs are often the key to the differences in efficiency between the private and public sectors. Public sector activities appear to be more vulnerable to the pressures which increase labor costs. The key factor here seems to be the ability of the public sector to pass on the results of labor agreements directly to the taxpayers who finance the activity. A private business does not have the same freedom, since prices have to be kept competitive. Thus, within the private sector there is a greater propensity to negotiate labor agreements with more concern for the effect on costs.

Private businesses are characterized by labor agreements which, for the most part, allow flexible use of labor in terms of skills and time. It is primarily in the public sector that restrictive work practices abound, that agreements specify that only certain classes of employees shall perform certain types of tasks, and that unions are able to limit work at unpopular hours for their members. Although the unions and the administrators are on opposite sides in labor negotiations, in the public sector it is easier for each to meet the other's needs. In the private sector the consumer is a tacit party to such agreements. If consumers do not accept the higher costs reflected in higher prices, they can take their trade elsewhere. In the public sector, the consumer is normally captive, having no other option to turn to.

The tendency toward uneconomic labor practices is a consequence of the monopoly which normally characterizes public operations, and the leverage it gives to unions. There are sectors of the private economy notable for unrealistic and uneconomic labor agreements. But these, too, tend to be in areas where monopoly or other special circumstance gives unions unusual power.

4. Capital costs

The degree of capitalization in the public sector depends on how much government has available to spend for this purpose. This depends, in turn, on the state of the national economy, on the levels of taxation which government thinks will be acceptable and on other demands on the public purse. Political pressures tend to deny public operations the degree of capitalization which they require.

For example, there is considerable political pressure to

squeeze capital spending in order to expand current spending. This is because the political pressures on current spending are huge. The labor force must be assuaged, and there must be few visible cuts in the services provided by public enterprise. Inevitably the capital side of the ledger suffers. Capital spending is less visible and has fewer interest groups to defend it. A capital cut only postpones the maintenance or acquisition of buildings and equipment. It is easier for legislators to raid the capital accounts.

The public sector is thus characterized by a tendency for current spending to rise as a proportion of total spending, and for the share devoted to capital to diminish. This means that the public sector of the economy often makes do with obsolete equipment. It is denied new, labor-saving and cost-cutting technology. The provision of improved and more valuable services are delayed, and the existing capital stock is made to last much longer than its planned life.

Against this standing tendency to skimp on capital spending in the public sector is the practice of capital renewal in the private sector. Unless firms keep up-to-date with developments, a rival may step in with a cheaper operation or a more valuable good or service and capture the market from those who lag behind. Sound business practices always involve adequate funding for the maintenance and acquisition of capital equipment. This is one reason why public operations often seem to be the poor relatives of their private counterparts.

5. Consumer input

The consumer is able to exercise a degree of control on private firms by deciding whether to shop with them or seek satisfaction elsewhere. The goods and services have to be oriented toward consumer satisfaction in order to attract customers and make profits. Where the public has no choice but to pay and take what is provided, as is usually the case in the public sector, this degree of control is absent.

Various expedients have been tried to achieve some substitute control. Boards representing consumers are often established with the statutory right to be consulted, or local committees of consumers may be part of the decision making process. In neither case does this give consumers the same power that the threat of withdrawal of trade does. In the absence of any effective input from consumers, public sector operations become producer-oriented and have their activities directed more toward meeting the interests of those engaged in production than toward those who receive the service.

Some public sector activities clearly are serving the interests of their workforce more than the interests of their customers. Often the hours of opening or availability of the service are directed toward accommodating the wishes of management and labor. Price and quality similarly reflect producer interests. In the case of public sector manufacturing, the central aim of the activity is often shifted from the production of goods for consumers to the provision of jobs for workers.

It is sadly ironic that private businesses are more under the control of the general public than those businesses which are 'publicly owned.' The former can be influenced directly and immediately by consumer decisions. The latter can only be influenced, if at all, over the vast distance of electoral control, and that in a diffuse and disorganized way.

6. Innovation and flexibility

When goods or services are produced under central direction, there is always a need to cope with the problem of control. Methods of production and distribution must be found which enable management to deal in manageable units. Not surprisingly, customers have to be dealt with in broad categories, rather than in terms of each consumer's individual preferences.

Where a number of competing firms vie for the attention of customers, much more variety is found and the consumer is more likely to find a service tailored to his or her individual needs. Private firms are constantly seeking new products and practices to give them a competitive edge. They adapt swiftly to changing market conditions, knowing that failure to do so might lead to bankruptcy.

The rate of innovation in public operations is much lower, and public services appear to change very slowly over time. During the time when a private sector good or service may change beyond recognition, the public sector seems to turn out the same products year after year. The low rate of innovation in the state's postal services, for example, contrasts sharply with the innovations of private postal services. Many other public sector activities also illustrate this point.

The desire to stretch public capital beyond the limit of its useful life, the reluctance of powerful public employee unions to accept change, and the absence of reward for entrepreneurial innovation all make for a public sector that is slower to adopt new ideas, more hidebound in its accustomed ways, and less adaptable to changing circumstances.

7. Decision making

Decisions in the private side of the economy are based heavily on economic factors. The choice of when to expand and where, the choice of a level of production, the choice of a price — all of these decisions are made on the basis of economic criteria. Firms have to gear their decision making to the market. They have to deal with the level of demand and with the price and availability of capital. And they have to use their knowledge of the market.

In the public sector many of the important decisions are made on political grounds. Private business inhabits the economic world, but state business lies in the political world and is governed accordingly. Decisions are made on the basis of factors such as the popularity of the government and how the decision will affect it. The number of marginal voting districts affected by a program can provide the basis for a decision to expand or contract it. Public tolerance of tax levels can determine the level of funding. Voter response to a price increase is an important factor in marketing.

What this means is that public sector decisions are divorced from the realities of supply and demand. Even a decision about the quantity to be produced is likely to be determined without reference to what is wanted. This, in turn, means that public sector services are not allocated to areas of greatest need, or where they will generate the greatest economic returns. Political objectives can only be pursued at the expense of economic ones. Inevitably, the public sector does not operate with the degree of efficiency achieved by the more market-directed private sector.

8. Condition of equipment

Public sector equipment, being 'publicly' owned, is not owned by anyone individually. As a result, few people treat it with the care and attention that they give to their own property. People protect their own property, and tend to keep equipment in good repair before damage allows it to deteriorate further. The obvious motive is the desire to avoid loss and expense. This motive is absent in respect of public sector property.

It may be sad to reflect that people will not care for common property as well as they care for individual property, but it seems to be a fact of life. It is one which militates against public equipment being in a good state of repair. Too often public equipment seems shoddy and badly maintained. Citizens who would object strongly to attacks on private property seem resigned to accept vandalism and ill-use of common goods. Again, there are the added effects of under-capitalization and a captive market. Both contrive to produce out-dated equipment in poor repair.

Private businesses tend to keep their equipment up to standard. To the private firm it is capital to be protected. Its condition affects both its use and the demand for it. Clean, modern and well-kept equipment is likely to increase sales and profit. This is why there is often the dramatic contrast between a private firm's gleaming facilities, clean and attractive, and the seedy, down-at-heel look of the public facilities.

9. Interruption of service

Although many goods and services were taken under the public wing in order that the supply might be guaranteed, a clear look at performance shows that the opposite is achieved. The public sector operation is more vulnerable to interruption.

Concentration of power provides the explanation. Public sector services in Britain are usually supplied by a public monopoly, with no alternative source of supply permitted. This, in turn, means that any interruption can shut down all sources of the service to consumers. In the private sector a labor dispute in one firm threatens only its own customers; a labor dispute in a public monopoly threatens everyone. This gives great power to the labor force. Given the many interests competing for public funds, it is almost inevitable that this power will be deployed from time to time as the labor force seeks to pursue its own financial interests.

In the private sector, the workforce always has to consider the effect of such actions on their jobs. A strike might cause a permanent loss of customers, forcing the firm out of business. In any case, the public always will be able to turn to non-striking competitors. Public sector monopoly, on the other hand, prevents a situation in which a strike is more attractive. The job is less at risk, the shutdown is total, and there is always the hope of public pressure on the employer (the government) to back down and restore the service.

Private sector delivery, then, promises considerably more security of service to the consumer than does public sector delivery. This applies to essential services just as much as to other services. Food distribution in Britain would be difficult to interrupt, because food is privately produced under conditions that are diverse and competitive. Water distribution, on the other hand, was recently interrupted by industrial action. Water, for the most part, is distributed by the public sector.

10. Responsiveness to cost control

Private sector costs are controlled competitively. They are not, in any case, financed out of taxation. A rise in the costs, and therefore in the price, of private goods or services leaves us the choice to turn to cheaper competitors, to take up substitutes, or to consume less. Private businesses have to be ever-alert to cost-cutting opportunities in order to attract financial capital. Investors put their money where the market indicates that a high return will be achieved. In the private sector funds are not diverted away from profitable and successful concerns and into inefficient or loss-making ones.

The public sector shows an immunity to cost controls. Its budget is nominally under the control of government, to be raised or lowered according to political decision. Yet government after government has attempted to control public sector costs without achieving any result commensurate with the effort expended.

The truth of the matter is that public sector costs are made up of a variety of factors, many of which are outside the control of government, even though technically within the legislative domain. Public servants have little interest in reducing costs. In fact, many have interests in the opposite direction. Groups which benefit from public operations form vociferous and effective lobby groups with high media visibility and the power to sap the will of an economy-minded administration.

The savings realized by cutting public sector costs rarely benefit those bureaucrats who are expected to do the cost cutting. Moreover, those who ultimately pay for public programs are neither as self-conscious nor as visible as those who benefit from them. All of this makes public sector costs very difficult to control. Attempted savings are more likely to result in the closure of the most popular and necessary aspect of the service, rather than achieve any savings from the elimination of administrative fat or from belt-tightening measures which improve efficiency.

The tendency in public sector operations is thus for a remorseless annual rise in costs, a rise which is beyond the powers of most governments to restrain, much less reverse. This brings in its wake a constant pressure on taxation, with funds needed for the expansion and development of successful private concerns being diverted and consumed by the inefficient state operation.

3. THE ATTEMPTS TO OVERCOME PUBLIC SECTOR PROBLEMS

Faced with the growing evidence of the deficiencies of public programs, governments have attempted a variety of expedient remedies. The structure of public monopoly often means that government must attempt to represent the interests of the consumer as well as those of itself, as producer. Since the consumer cannot go elsewhere if dissatisfied, government is obliged to take due note of complaints, and to attempt remedies.

The problem arises from the fact that any proposed improvements in public services always seem to be those which cost more money. The industry itself goes to great lengths to show that only a large influx of new public money would enable it to deal with its shortcomings. Government thus finds itself in the position of attempting to stem the drain on taxpayers' resources, yet facing demands for improved services which would consume yet more funds.

If services become poorer because funds are restricted, the level of complaints will rise. On the other hand, if more money is allocated, there will be a greater burden on taxpayers, including the wealth-creating private economy. Government finds itself caught in the jaws of a vice which severely restricts any freedom of action.

For many years there was a tendency in the advanced economies to respond to social problems by allocating more money to public programs. In some countries this practice continues. The comparison of public and private operations suggests, however, that there are weaknesses inherent in public sector organizations which lead to comparatively ineffective use of funds. The tendency to skimp on capital spending provides a case in point. As their capital is depleted, public programs appeal for more capital funding. Unfortunately, the forces which lead to unbalanced current spending are still there, and any new funds are subject to the same one-sided pull. As a result, the proportion of any new allocation which reaches the capital account will be small. The logic that directs the system will cause much of the new funding to go toward relieving the pressure and allowing a continuation of an excessive use of labor and a top-heavy administration.

PROBLEMS OF PRESENT TACTICS

There are four tactics used from time to time by governments to deal with escalating costs of public programs. Unfortunately, none of these poses a solution to the inherent problems.

1. Efficiency drives

When governments become aware of the inferior performance of public sector supply, the attempt is sometimes made to graft onto the public program some of the efficiency-making expertise of the private sector. Typically in Britain, a senior management executive will head an efficiency program, promising to use in the public sector the same methods which bring success in streamlining private companies. Sometimes a group of observers with considerable private sector expertise will conduct an investigation and study, identifying areas where efficiency could be improved and making the appropriate recommendations. Whether the private manager is brought in from outside to run it, or whether he is asked to examine and report in the role of outside observer, the attempt is the same. It is an attempt to use the methods which the private sector induces spontaneously because of its need to remain competitive and profitable. Yet these methods are not induced in the same way in the public sector because it is non-competitive and non profit-making by design.

The effort is commendable, but of temporary effect. Such campaigns have achieved limited success, but only during a short period of public pressure. When the novelty has died, the orthodox practices of the public sector gradually reassert their effects. The history of the public sector in Britain is littered with the names of 'whiz-kids' who brought a beneficial but short-lived influence from the private sector.

The reason for the transient nature of any improvement lies in the fact that streamlined business practices are an outgrowth of streamlined business. One can introduce bulk buying, better cash-flow control and various short-cut procedures, but the one thing difficult to introduce is the incentive which will sustain and extend those practices. In the private sector it is the pursuit of profit itself which ultimately serves that end.

It might be possible to introduce into bureaucracies schemes designed to substitute for the profit incentive. Ways might be found of linking the fate and fortunes of individual administrators with the performance of their area of responsibility. But the practice calls to mind the habit in socialist economies of allowing a miniscule market to survive in order to establish prices, or of paying a production bonus to factories or workers who exceed the government-imposed quotas. In neither case is this as effective as the real thing. It resembles the private enterprise economy only as a candle resembles the sun.

2. Drives to eliminate waste

A frequent tactic employed by a cost-conscious government is the initiation of procedures to identify and eliminate waste within public operations. An outsider is brought in, as with the efficiency drive. But in campaigns against waste another civil servant is often brought in to take a detached look at spending. The aim is to eliminate flagrant sources of abuse, some so habitual that they no longer are recognized by those within the department.

In the drive to cut waste, attention often focuses on trivial items, such as requiring bureaucrats to stay in three-star hotels instead of five-star hotels, or requiring the re-use of standardized envelopes. The more serious aim of these reviews is to pare down the administrative fat which adheres to the meat of public programs, without cutting the service itself. If more productive use can be made of administrative personnel, then the hope is that spending can be curbed without risk to the program's output.

Broadly speaking, such reviews have a propensity to instate

a freeze on hiring, and to merge several departments so that one establishment can take responsibility for several activities.

As with efficiency campaigns, the drive against waste achieves temporary results. The larger department can indeed handle more areas and in the short term reduce overhead costs. The problem is that the new, enlarged department has more authority and importance than its predecessors, and has more ability to allocate increased responsibility, and increased funding, to itself. Inevitably, it acquires enhanced status with each new responsibility, and its administrators move up the scale of prestige and salary. Being larger, it is often even *more* difficult to manage.

There is another effect which the anti-waste drive shares with the efficiency campaign. Both try to bring in a fresh look from outside. In doing so, both undermine administrative morale by having key decisions taken outside of the department's own structure. Civil servants speak of 'riding out' these campaigns, waiting for less stringent times to return, or for a government more relaxed about public spending.

3. Eliminating unnecessary programs

Governments seeking to cut taxes look for areas of public sector supply rendered obsolete and unnecessary by changing social circumstances. A body set up half a century ago might no longer be required, given the new levels of affluence. The steam laundries and public bath-houses of Victorian England might be no longer needed, now that most homes have bathrooms and washing machines and coin-operated laundries are easily accessible.

A possible source of public sector saving might be found in the complete elimination of unnecessary services. The problem for government lies in the determination of what is or is not necessary. Administrations which embark on such a course are frequently surprised to discover just how passionate and vociferous is the defense for any public program, no matter how useless it might now seem.

The point is that every public service has its beneficiaries. There are some who have a locational advantage in a tax-funded program of little general benefit. There are regular users who prefer the free or cheap service, even though they could afford the private sector alternatives. The steam laundries and bath-houses provide examples. Whenever there are moves to close any of them, a public outcry is always the result.

Every public program also has its losers. These are usually the general taxpayers, whose standard of living is lowered to provide the service which benefits others. These losers are neither well organized nor very visible. Those who benefit from public programs know themselves to be beneficiaries. They are a visible group ready to lobby and attract media attention. Rare is the general taxpayer who is prepared to chain himself to the railings of a bath-house demanding its closure to save public funds. Pressure upon legislators is heavily loaded in support of public programs, no matter how little good the programs create.

Administrators themselves, although expected to oversee the dissolution of unnecessary programs, have no interest in seeing this done successfully. On the contrary, it threatens their status and even their job to have their area of responsibility diminished. Not surprisingly, all kinds of bureaucratic obstacles and impediments appear in the way of policies which would phase out public programs.

These effects take their toll. Governments which embark boldly on elimination of useless activities soon find there are none to be agreed upon. Every program is fought for bitterly, with losses in prestige and goodwill sacrificed in return for only meager gains. The steam runs out of the government drive long before it successfully shuts down the publicly-funded Victorian laundry.

4. Cash limits

The policy of cash limits is the outcome of an intelligent attempt to cut the Gordian knot of departmental spending. In annual budget preparations, governments have seen each element of the public sector fought for by its own administrators, with the cumulative effect being an overall increase in spending.

The cash limits strategy tries to do two things. By imposing an overall budget limit on a department, it encourages some areas within the department to oppose spending by others, since this is the only way their own can acquire additional funds. The hope is that in this way, essential services will be guaranteed but that administrators will join forces with each other to vote down increased appropriations to unnecessary activities. The second aim of a cash limits policy is that the administrators themselves will introduce efficiency and anti-waste campaigns to continue operation under the constraint of an overall limit on spending. Here too, the assumption is that what is not needed will go, leaving an altogether more cost-effective program.

Neither attempt succeeds as intended, leaving the policy of cash limits much less successful at controlling public spending than its proponents hoped. In the first place, within a department it is not the most necessary programs which corner the funding, but the ones with greatest political pull. Departments of state are no less vulnerable to office politics than other organizations. The difference here is that public money is tied up in it. Sometimes the large bureau has more influence because it is larger; so the effect of cash limit campaigns is to improve the position of the big bureaucratic operations at the expense of the smaller ones.

Secondly, the effect of the overall limit on each operation is by no means that which is sought. Instead of the savings coming from the elimination of inefficiency and waste, spending cuts tend to be applied directly to the delivery of valuable services. Administrators asked to economize do not do so with their own jobs and salaries. They come forward instead with proposals to cut out certain parts of the service, albeit without significant reductions in overhead costs. The effect of cash limits, therefore, is to make the public sector *less* efficient. Capital spending is cut first, being the easiest option. Then important services are dropped leaving roughly the same overhead establishment operating on a smaller capital base with lower output.

The other aspect of cash limits which is distressing to government is the degree to which media manipulation is used to undermine the campaign. Those inside and outside the bureaucracy who oppose limits on spending know which are the most popular and sensitive services. These are the ones put at risk first or characterized as being most vulnerable. Savings on the welfare program can only be achieved, it seems, by closing schools for handicapped children and by throwing dependent old people out onto the street. Naturally enough, these horror stories are extensively covered by the media, ably assisted by leaked memoranda showing more atrocities on the way. Government supporters in the legislature wilt under the hail of fire, and the cash limit campaign has its fangs pulled.

CONCLUSION

The failure of these four tactics suggests that government is unable to control public sector spending except temporarily in a few selected areas and at great cost in political support.

Although criticisms of administrations abound from those opposed to public sector spending, lack of effort on the part of the administration is not usually a just charge. Complaints that the government 'was not tough enough', 'should have done more', or 'ought to have done it all on the first day while it was still popular' — all assume that government *can* control public sector spending. Failure to do so, it is assumed, must involve a failure of will. Yet the above analysis suggests that public spending is pushed by factors outside the control of government. It is the critics who are at fault, adhering to the myth of legislative omnipotence. A careful and sympathetic examination of the forces which thwart the intentions of government might point the way to policies which could overcome them.

4. DISMANTLING THE STATE

All of the policies which attempt to control public sector costs operate at the macro level, attempting to secure solutions from the top. All of them operate on the supply side, seeking to alter the conditions under which public sector goods and services are produced. All of them seek wide-ranging benefits secured by a series of changes imparted through central planning. All of them fail, to a greater or lesser extent, to achieve the chosen objectives.

There is, however, an alternative approach which was hardly featured in the manifesto of the Conservative government elected in Britain in 1979, but which has nonetheless achieved major successes. This is the policy of moving state operations toward the private sector, instead of merely attempting to restrain their costs. The thinking behind this approach is that only the private sector itself can impose the economic disciplines and create the incentives which are desperately needed.

The policy of *privatization*, of transferring public activities wholly or partly into the private sector, derives from a recognition that the weaknesses of the public supply are inherent. It assumes that any temporary grafting of private enterprise attributes onto the state sector will be temporary, and that the gains will be whittled away as the characteristics of the public economy reassert themselves. The attempts to make the public sector more cost-effective and more responsive to demand are ones which must be continually remade, at great cost in political goodwill, and with no permanent success.

The actual *transfer* to the private sector, on the other hand, can take the service into the purely economic world and out of the political world. It can expose the service to the perpetual effects of competition and cost controls. It can give consumers choice and input. It can leave capital spending and price decisions free to be determined by straightforward economic logic, instead of by an anticipation of what the public might tolerate.

The transfer of resources

From the point of view of government, perhaps the most attractive feature of this solution is its permanence. It needs to be done only once, whereas the cost campaigns need to be fought and refought, year after year. Once the service is in the private sector, it is outside the direct area of government responsibility. Its costs no longer have a direct impact on taxation; its labor force no longer works for the state; and its level of service is determined by demand.

Of nearly equal importance to government is that cost-cutting campaigns are normally equated with cuts in services, whereas the movement of a public operation into the private economy need not involve any deterioration in quality of service. On the contrary, many of the forces which contribute to sub-standard performance by state enterprises will cease to operate after the transfer is made, and an improvement in quality can be expected. In political terms this means that a government which adopts this approach faces less public criticism and media denigration than one pursuing economy campaigns perceived as a threat to essential services.

The policy of transferring operations from the public to the private economy is much more oriented to the demand side than to the supply side. It asks the fundamental question of a state activity: can public demand for this service be satisfied by the private market? If the answer is yes, then a variety of measures are available for effecting that transfer. Many of the actual methods of making the change occur piecemeal, allowing separate decisions to build up gradually to the transfer of an entire sector.

None of this should imply that privatization is easy. Just as there is no shortage of people urging the government to cut costs, so there is no lack of those recommending privatization. But there is no such profusion of people explaining *how* costs can be cut, or how tasks which have for many years been performed in the state sector can suddenly be incorporated into the private and competitive economy. In practice, the shift of supply from state to private sector requires a battery of sophisticated techniques which take full account of the political and social problems of the public sector, as well as of its economic shortcomings.

The Conservative government in Britain, which was elected in 1979 and re-elected in 1983, has used more than twenty-two different methods of transferring public operations wholly or partially into the private sector. In doing so, it has achieved the largest transfer of property since the dissolution of the monasteries under King Henry VIII, a transfer from the state to its citizens. This transfer has meant that large and increasing areas of public supply are now subject to the economic disciplines brought by the private market. From the government's point of view, costs now are being controlled more securely than could ever be achieved through economy campaigns.

The transfer is almost certainly permanent. It has been achieved using a variety of ways which make it difficult to reverse. New groups have a vested interest in the new status quo, and a public accustomed to regarding the public sector as a drain on its resources is unlikely to give endorsement to a campaign for re-appropriation. The transfer is ongoing. A small part of the total public sector has been privatized, but the techniques which have worked on one area are constantly being prepared for application elsewhere. The progress is remorseless and one-way.

These continuing changes have some similarities with the great retreat of government which was set in motion in the first half of the nineteenth century in Britain. Under the influence of the ideas expounded by Adam Smith, a succession of administrations dismantled much of the regulatory apparatus of state over a period of half a century, culminating with the repeal of the corn laws in 1846.

In recent times, the year 1979 appears to have denoted the high-water mark of the public sector in Britain. Since then, much of the huge machine of state industries, regulations and transfer payments has systematically been dismantled, and replaced by more efficient and more responsive private sector alternatives.

What this means for Britain, among many other things, is that the potential for future governments which are less economy-minded is being severely restricted. An administration which merely holds down the growth of government for a time is eventually easily replaced by another big spender. This time, however, there has been a permanent transfer of resources, and a momentum generated which will be difficult for successor governments to withstand. Britain may well be entering upon the early stages of another long retreat by government.

Wide range of methods

One reason for the success of this strategy has been the wide range of techniques used to execute the transfers. It is not simply a question of 'selling off the state.' On the contrary, there are very few parts of the public sector which are appropriate for direct sale. It is a question of regarding each part of the state as an individual problem requiring appropriate treatment.

The successful methods have been those which deal with the entrenched forces, with the interest groups and with the political pressures which devolve on the state sector. For every state program there are the administrators whose job is enhanced in status by the responsibility for it. There are the public sector labor unions which thrive on the power of a public service monopoly. There is the workforce with a guaranteed job for which they have often been able to secure comfortable conditions without the risks of bankruptcy to restrain them. There are those who benefit from a subsidized operation, and those who thrive by representing and lobbying for those recipients. And there are the media, ever-ready to see government failing in its responsibilities.

These groups have the potential to oppose a transfer to the private sector, just as they are able to thwart cost-cutting exercises. The successful methods of transfer involve a recognition of the role played by each of these groups, and the inclusion of provisions which neutralize or outweigh the adverse effect they might have. If, for example, circumstances are contrived in which the beneficiaries do even better under a private system, their voice will be muted, alongside those of their lobbyists and the media. Their embrace of the new system may be sufficient to outweigh the objections of the bureaucracy and the labor unions. Alternatively, ways might be devised to ensure that the change was accompanied by an improvement for the workforce. Each of the methods employed successfully has its own variation for coping with the realities.

For government, a very important factor in the change from public to private is the need for assurances that the most vulnerable and dependent groups will be protected through the turnover. The vocabulary of labor union opponents of privatization abounds with terms which imply that the weakest will go to the wall. Profit-seeking entrepreneurs will move in, it is claimed, 'skimming off' the lucrative and profitable parts of the service, leaving those without power without a service. The concept is erroneous because it takes no account of the remarkable ability of private businesses to move in and make money from services which cost the state a heavy loss. Yet, it still leaves government seeking to build assurances that dependent groups will not suffer because of the transfer. Some of the techniques therefore involve granting dependent groups buying power, either by direct grants to needy individuals, or through the use of publicly-paid contractors to guarantee the service for them.

In the case of utilities and services deemed essential, a government contemplating a switch to private sector supply might need to give considerable attention to the problem of outlying consumers, and take steps to ensure that supply can be guaranteed to these consumers after the change. Sometimes the removal of unnecessary regulation suffices to ensure that new types of service will evolve which can profitably serve even remote or scattered customers. Sometimes more active assurances might be granted through the charters of private companies seeking to operate.

It is by careful examination of the processes of the public sector that government is able to anticipate the response of the various parties involved, and to make the necessary adjustments to the techniques to be used. The process of privatization is not one which depends only on the will of a government. There must also be considerable creativity in policy innovation. New and sometimes intricate techniques are required, each to be tailored to the particular problems caused by individual areas of public supply. Public ownership cannot be dealt with by the same methods as public regulation. State-produced goods require different techniques for transfer than those needed for the transfer of state-produced services.

The operations of the public sector have to be regarded as processes, and examined minutely to track down the way in which their elements motivate individuals involved as producers or consumers, as taxpayers or beneficiaries. Policy creativity is needed to ensure that the new reality will be willingly supported by enough of its participants to make it a success, and to guarantee its permanence. *Micropolitics* is the art of generating circumstances in which individuals will be motivated to prefer and embrace the alternative of private supply, and in which people will make individual and voluntary decisions whose cumulative effect will be to bring about the desired state of affairs. The process of transfer from public to private economy is most securely achieved when its progress is evolutionary, arising from free decisions.

The following is an analysis of the various methods employed to dismantle the state. Each deals in a different way with the problems posed by various interest groups. The analysis covers many different types of public operations and reveals many different types of solutions.

5. THE TECHNIQUES

METHOD ONE: SELLING THE WHOLE

There are cases of public sector activity in which government is able to sell, as a unit, the whole of a specific operation. Relatively small organizations which deal with a specialized product or service are often suitable for this very direct treatment. Alternatively, units which have been acquired by chance, as subsidiaries of larger concerns which were nationalized, can sometimes be returned to the private sector by this method.

Large parts of the state economy are not suitable for direct sale, however. Those involving regulation or transfer payments cannot be run as profit-making enterprises, and many of those engaged in the production of goods or services have a long history of financial losses and labor troubles which render them unattractive to buyers. The argument is sometimes advanced that government enterprises which make losses cannot be sold, while charges of 'asset-stripping' are levelled at attempts to sell enterprises that are profitable. The argument is more valid if it is inverted. Operations which make profits can be sold, and those which make losses must be sold in order to stop the constant drain on resources. While some state operations make money, it is usually caused by very temporary circumstances, and should prompt politicians to move quickly toward their disposal while conditions are good.

A sale, skillfully handled, creates a new interest group in the new owners. The group constitutes a lobby which can be counted on to oppose moves towards subsequent expropriation. With the prospect of private capital coming in to develop and renew the operation, the workforce may have any initial misgivings allayed, and come rapidly to prefer working for a successful private concern rather than for an ailing, capital-starved public organization. The bottom-line security in the state system may be shown to be worth less to them than the opportunities for advancement which a streamlined, modernized private company can bring them.

In a similar way, any initial doubts felt by the public concerning the possible risk to supply can be replaced by a conviction that the new service is better, more varied and more responsive. In any event, the areas where total sale is appropriate are often those in which the consumers form a highly visible special interest group. The effect on the general public may be minimal with respect to their role as taxpayers. The proceeds of the sale go to relieve the pressures on the public purse. They can be deployed to reduce the public borrowing, to narrow a deficit or to reduces taxes.

In light of these incentives taxpayers and legislators can be added to the groups who can gain substantially from the sale of a public operation. Under the right circumstances a direct sale can be achieved with political as well as financial success, and it can be made practically impossible to reverse.

Amersham International

A good example was afforded in Britain by the sale of Amersham International, the small radionics firm. Previously known as the Radiochemical Centre, Amersham International had dealt for forty years in the supply of man-made radioactive materials obtained from nuclear reactors. More recently it had developed strong links with the market for extremely sophisticated medical equipment.

Until the offer for sale on February 15, 1982 the shares were held by the government's Atomic Energy Authority. The price per share was £1.42, and the offer for sale was oversubscribed 24.6 times, with applications from both employees and the general public. The employees were allocated 1.8 million shares (representing 3.6 percent of the total) and 99 percent of them took the government offer of £50 worth of free shares. Furthermore, over 80 percent of employees took up the one-to-one share offer, whereby their own money would be matched by an equivalent number of free shares worth approximately £250 per applicant. Also, 40 percent of the employees applied to buy under a preferential application scheme.

In the end, the sale raised £71 million, taking into consideration the £310,000 that was paid for professional advice. Of this £71 million, £5.7 million will eventually go to the company while the remainder will go to the government.

Amersham International was wholly sold off. It is now fully within the private sector of the economy. The method of sale was criticized in Parliament, with allegations that the low offer price had enabled friends of the government to 'make a killing.' This may have precipitated subsequent moves towards sale of shares by other methods.

METHOD TWO: SELLING COMPLETE PARTS OF THE WHOLE

Even where the whole of a public operation cannot be sold, there are instances in which distinct sections of the whole may be sold off independently. Even though the main body may be in no condition to attract buyers, it may be possible to separate out parts of the organization which have better prospects of finding purchasers. In some cases two or more parts may be effectively packaged, making a parcel that is a viable proposition for a purchaser.

When the whole of a public sector organization is sold, it tends to be sold by the issue of shares on the stock market. Thus, when a public enterprise is sold en bloc, there is a great deal of attention paid to the method of issue, the ways of bidding for shares, and the diversity of ownership which is sought.

When a complete part of the whole is offered for sale, it is usually done by finding a single private buyer. For this kind of sale it is usual for negotiations to be undertaken with interested parties, such as corporations already active in similar fields. Price and conditions are agreed, and the transfer is effected in exchange for payment from the company to the government. In this way, complete parts of state activities are taken over by corporations operating within the private economy. Very often, these activities were anomalous to the main activity to which they originally belonged.

Sometimes the government has actively sought buyers, and carefully prepared packages for the purpose of enticing sales. In other cases, with a government known to be sympathetic to the concept of privatization, the initiative has come from the potential buyer. In this case a corporation may approach the government with a suggestion for take-over.

When parts are sold to a single buyer, the outcome for the employees, including those at management level, is of the utmost importance. Without a diversified ownership there is no broad-based new interest group to defend the new status quo. In this case it is advantageous to have a management and workforce who perceive the new arrangement as beneficial to themselves. This at once removes a possible source of opposition to the transfer, while simultaneously helping to make the change permanent. The new owners, of course, have an interest in protecting the new arrangement, and the taxpayers benefit from the proceeds of the sale.

As with the sale of entire operations, the expectation for the sale of a part is that the service will improve as it is modernized and recapitalized, and that consumers will prefer it in its new setting, offering yet more resistance to any attempted or proposed reversal of the change.

Range of examples

The success of this method is illustrated by the wide variety of state operations which have been returned to the private sector by its use. The following list shows the diversity of its application.

(1) Rail hotels. The sale of hotels owned by British Rail illustrates the device of selling off units as separate entities. It seems strange to think of a state-run railroad being in the hotel business, but British Rail had found itself operating twenty-nine hotels. By March 1983, twenty-seven out of the twenty-nine hotels had been privatized by the British Rail Board subsidiary, British Rail Investments. Three Scottish hotels were placed into a new company, Gleneagles Hotels Ltd, which started to trade in June 1981. The British Rail Board received £10.35 million — part of it in deferred payment — of which £4.5 million was used to buy loanstock and shares in the company.

In February 1983, bids for a total of £25.85 million were accepted for ten hotels and then another nine were sold soon after for £8.7 million. (The two remaining hotels have been let on short leases and not sold, because they were in the immediate locality of stations shortly awaiting development.)

(2) English Channel ferry services. Shipping ferry services across the English Channel were another subsidiary of the state railroad company. When they were formed into a separate state-owned company in 1979, the name 'Sealink' was chosen. It was one of Europe's largest ferry groupings, operating forty ships on twenty-three different routes, and owning seven major harbors, together with several smaller harbors and piers.

The British government decided to sell Sealink to a single buyer, and in 1984 it was sold to Sea Containers, a Bermuda-based American company, for £66 million.

(3) The Manpower Services Commission. Britain's Manpower Services Commission has responsibilities which include job advertising and some industrial training. A number of the restaurants in its training centers have been sold off, thus taking them outside the public sector. The Commission is to close large numbers of its employment exchanges (called job centers), and use kiosks in private premises such as supermarkets to take their place.

(4) North Sea oilfields. The North Sea oilfields, which were government-owned through the state-run gas corporation, were formed into a company called Enterprise Oil. Stock was offered to the public in June, 1984, at £1.85 per share, representing a total valuation of £392 million. Investors took only 65 percent of the stock issue, but the government received all its money because the underwriters took the rest. The low demand was attributed to several factors, including a low prospective yield, an unsettled oil market, and rising interest rates.

(5) Government land and buildings. Sales of land and buildings by both the British government and the city and district governments have taken place at an increasing rate.

(6) Tractors and trucks. The state-run car industry in Britain, British Leyland, sold its forklift truck subsidiary and its tractor line in Bathgate, Scotland.

(7) Refrigerators. British Leyland also ran a state-owned refrigerator company called Prestcold. This was sold to Suter Electrical, a private company, for £9 million.

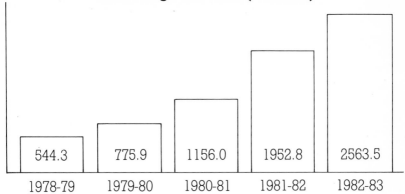

Table 1
Sale of land and buildings by central
and local government (£ million)

544.3	775.9	1156.0	1952.8	2563.5
1978-79	1979-80	1980-81	1981-82	1982-83

(8) The National Coal Board. The state-run National Coal Board in Britain sold land, vehicles and buildings to the tune of £19 million.

(9) British Airways. The state airline, British Airways, sold off a subsidiary communications company called International Aeradio, for £60 million. This was while British Airways itself was being prepared for privatization.

(10) Freeway service areas. The British Department of Transport has sold thirty-eight state-run freeway service areas which provided motorists with automobile service, refueling and catering facilities. They were sold on fifty-year leases to the Rank Organization, Granada, Trusthouse Forte and Imperial Foods for roughly £50 million.

(11) Oil stockpiles. British government-owned oil stockpiles were sold in 1982-83 for a yield of £33 million.

(12) Oil and gas exploration licences. For the eighth round of offshore licensing for oil and gas exploration, the British government decided to sell licences for fifteen of the 184 off-shore areas. Offers for seven of these raised nearly £33 million.

(13) Water authority land. The state-run Regional Water Authorities in Britain sold off £3 million-worth of land in 1979-80.

(14) Property Services Agency. The Property Service Agency administers state-owned estates in Britain. It sold land

and buildings worth £5 million in 1979-80, and a further £4 million worth in 1980-81.

(15) British Steel. The government-run steel industry in Britain, British Steel, sold a subsidiary steel company called Redpath Dorman Long to Trafalgar House, a private corporation.

(16) British Sugar. The state's holding of 24 percent of the stock in British Sugar was finally disposed of in 1982, with the government gaining £44 million from the sale to the private sector.

(17) Crown Agents. The Crown Agents, responsible for administering overseas real estate held by Britain, sold over £16 million worth of assets in Australia.

(18) National Health Service land. The National Health Service in Britain is reckoned to be Europe's largest employer. It also holds large amounts of land. For the two years ending in March 1981, it sold 1,460 acres for a total of £25.5 million. A further 4,000 acres are currently awaiting sale back to the private sector, since the National Health Service has declared it no longer needs them.

(19) British Petroleum. British Petroleum was an oil company which had the British government as a majority stockholder. However, in November 1979, the government reduced its holding from 51 percent to 46 percent. This meant that the company was now technically in the private sector, and could raise capital without it being counted as government borrowing. A subsequent stock issue of 1981 lowered the government holding to 39 percent, and the government sold some of its stock in 1984 for £565 million, bringing its holding down to 31.7 percent of the stock.

(20) Property in the New Towns. Britain's 'New Towns' were set up as government-sector corporations, mostly after World War II. Since 1979, the first year of the Thatcher Administration, the New Towns have sold £400 million worth of industrial and commercial assets. In addition, the New Towns have sold large quantities of land for residential use, as well as actual homes. For the years 1981-83, sales amounted to 75 hectares (1 hectare = 2.5 acres), land made available under licence came to 580 hectares, and dwellings sold totalled 13,960.

(21) Local government residential land. Britain's local authorities, the regional and district governments, similarly disposed of residential land. Over the same period, 1981-83, they sold 1,615 hectares of land for private housing and made a further 470 hectares available for disposal later on.

(22) Shipbuilding. The state shipbuilding company, British Shipbuilders, sold off its biggest loss-making yard, called the Scott-Lithgow Shipyard. It was sold for £12 million to Trafalgar House, with payment being made in installments. The government had to spend £71 million to 'wipe the slate clean,' writing off debts and honoring commitments. This sounds like a bad deal until one appreciates that Scott-Lithgow lost £66 million in 1982-83 alone. It was a case of short-term spending to free the state from long-term losses.

(23) Suez Finance Company. In 1980-81 the government received £22 million from the sale of its shares in the Suez Finance Company.

(24) The Forestry Commission. The Forestry Commission is responsible for the huge state-owned forests in Britain. It has sold tracts of land and property, including residential properties. The new 1981 Forestry Act allowed it to sell both planted and unplanted land.

METHOD THREE: SELLING A PROPORTION OF THE WHOLE OPERATION

Where it is inappropriate to offer the whole activity for sale, or even dispose of distinct parts of it, it is sometimes feasible to offer for sale a proportion of the operation. In common parlance, this means allowing people to buy in on a state business, while retaining a proportion of it in public ownership. Instead of offering 100 percent of it for sale, the government offers a smaller percentage, often 51 percent.

There are clear advantages to the government in following this course of action. In the first place, it makes money from the sale. Secondly, it spreads ownership and reduces the size of the public economy. By the British Treasury's own regulations, if the state holding drops below 50 percent, future capital raising by the business is exempted from the public sector borrowing requirements and capital may be raised on normal commercial considerations. But even if only 10 percent is sold to the private market, the business becomes subject to many of the laws which protect the owners of private corporations.

From the government's point of view, this can be a very effective method of gaining value for money when releasing government assets. A state corporation with an unhappy history behind it might not command a very high price. By selling a percentage, especially a controlling percentage, the state returns it to the private sector even when it retains a significant holding. As the disciplines of the private sector assert their effect on the operation, it becomes more cost-effective and more profitable. The value of the state's holding increases, and can be sold for a higher price.

The sale of a proportion of the total ownership brings in immediate cash to the government, and to the business itself for recapitalization. It sometimes turns what is in most years a liability to the government into a substantial asset. There is a reasonable expectation that the improved performance will increase the worth of the state's remaining percentage to one which approaches or exceeds that of the original whole.

Naturally enough, the new shareholders who have bought stock form a group opposed to subsequent expropriation. Management and workforce can be brought to appreciate their improved prospects under an influx of private capital. Legislators gain in many of the ways outlined. As with other methods of sale, it is the public sector unions — leadership rather than membership — which form the single group which can be expected to oppose the measure. They stand to lose the power which their position in the public sector gives them, and which will be limited by all kinds of commercial considerations in the private sector.

Britoil

A British example of this type of exercise is afforded by the sale of 51 percent of the shares in Britoil. This was the name given to the state activity which deals with the exploration for, and production of, oil and gas from the North Sea.

Britoil's assets included six producing oil fields and one producing gas field. In addition to this it held three more oil fields with very good potential, but still under development. At the time of its share offer (1983) it had the largest acreage of licence interests in the United Kingdom Continental Shelf area and was responsible for approximately seven per cent ot the total oil production from that area.

The sale offer for Britoil, of up to 255 million ordinary shares of 10p each at a minimum price of £2.15 per share, was made on November 19, 1982. This represented 51 percent of the shares in Britoil and led to applications being received for around 70 million shares. This undersubscription left the remainder, 185 million, in the hands of the underwriters and sub-underwriters.

Of all applications received, 99 percent came from small investors and employees, with over 35,000 applications being for 2,000 shares or less. This may be explained partially by a small bonus scheme which involved the 'gift' of further shares if the shareholders retain their holding until November 30, 1985. The net result was that 92 percent of eligible employees bought over 500,000 shares.

The total share issue grossed over £548 million, and the gross proceeds to the government will eventually reach around £640 million when the £88 million debenture is repaid by Britoil.

The commonly accepted reasons why the share issue was so undersubscribed are the considerable uncertainty over oil prices and the belief (since proven correct) that they were about to fall from 1982 levels, and the fact that the method of sale — inviting bids for shares in an auction-style arrangement — is far too inflexible. Doubts about this method explain why subsequent sales have been by fixed-price offer.

Despite the undersubscription for the stock, the government (and hence the public) received their money from the underwriters. The sale was not only successful insofar as it is desirable to have satisfied investors participating, but also in terms of the large number of investors who have gained from the privatization operation, as the government intended.

Cable and Wireless

A second example of a partial sale is illustrated by Cable and Wireless, a state-run communications company. Under the provisions of the 1981 Telecommunications Act the British government was empowered to sell shares in Cable and

Wireless. It was a group of companies who, in the main, operated overseas, supplying telecommunications services and facilities. However, since its semi-privatization it has attempted to shift towards the British market. To that end it provided 40 percent of the initial finance for Mercury, the newly licensed telecommunications firm which is establishing an independent system in competition with British Telecom. Cable and Wireless had interests in the provision and operation of the public telecommunications services of thirty different countries and territories.

Following the offer for sale, the government held 50.53 percent of the issued share capital of the company. Meanwhile, over 99 percent of the workforce decided to buy 3,785,833 shares — equivalent to 5 percent of the proportion of total issued share capital. However, the government's share fell to 45 percent when a subsequent issue to existing stockholders in March 1983 was not taken up by the government, thus increasing the proportion of Cable and Wireless shares held in the private sector to 55 percent. This state of circumstances did not last very long. On October 27, 1983 the government announced that it intended to sell even more of its remaining shareholding in Cable and Wireless plc — about half, representing 22.2 percent of the company's issued ordinary share capital.

The sale was made at a minimum price of £2.75 a share, with a total of 100 million shares on offer. The government was guaranteed a minimum of £275 million following the completion of the underwriting on November 25, 1983, but exactly how much will end up in the coffers has yet to be announced, since the costs involved in the sale are still to be calculated.

A further 25 percent of the government's holding in Cable and Wireless was sold in early 1984, raising £262 million. This means that the government now retains only 25 percent of the total stock.

Associated British Ports

The state-owned harbors were sold by a similar method. The British Transport Docks Board operated the following ports: Southampton, Hull, Grimsby, Immingham, Goole, Swansea,

Port Talbot, Barry, Cardiff, Newport, King's Lynn, Lowestoft, Plymouth (Millbay Dock only), Garston, Fleetwood, Barrow, Silloth, Ayr, and Troon — a total of nineteen in all, dealing primarily with freight traffic.

After its conversion into Associated British Ports, a total of 21.3 million shares were sold in February 1983. This represented 51.5 percent of the total shares of the company, with the remaining 48.5 percent being retained by the government. All in all, 91 percent of the employees became shareholders, buying a total of 1.7 million shares (12.2 percent of the total). The government offered shares at £1.12 each but they were oversubscribed 33 times. Nevertheless, it received £21.95 million from the sale as gross proceeds, plus a further £25 million in cash from the Associated British Ports group. The government finally dissolved itself from ABP when, on 18 April 1984, it sold 19.4 million shares of common stock, representing the remaining 48.5 percent of the company's stock. Gross proceeds were £53 million.

British Aerospace

British Aerospace (BAe), established as a state-owned corporation in 1977, manufactures aircraft and aircraft components.

By 1980, BAe had established itself as a sizeable concern, with capital assets of about £700 million, a profit in the same period of around £65 million, and a workforce of 75,000 employees. It is mainly involved in the civilian side of the industry, with interests in Airbus Industries, the A310 aircraft, and older, better-known models such as the BAe 111 aircraft. Significantly, the Airbus family has been said to represent the only credible competitor to the American giant civil aircraft manufacturers, such as Boeing, McDonnell-Douglas and Lockheed. However, BAe is also involved on the military side of aircraft production, with its highly profitable aerospace and missile interests plus its joint ventures such as the Tornado, the Harrier Jump Jet, and the Anglo-French Jaguar aircraft.

In 1981, on February 13, the Secretary of State for Industry offered for sale up to 100 million shares (representing 51.6 percent of the company's commons stock) at a price of £1.50

each. Over 27,000 employees bought shares (40 percent of the total workforce) and, in fact, applied for around 10.6 million, while only receiving 7.1 million. This represented an employee over-subscription of about 50 percent.

The gross receipts from the sale were approximately £148.6 million, but after deducting the expenses of the sale (£5.6 million) and payments to the company of £100 million for the new shares subscribed for by the Secretary of State, total net receipts were £42.9 million.

Jaguar — British Leyland

Britain's state-owned carmaker, British Leyland, announced that 177.9 million shares in Jaguar, its luxury division, would be sold at £1.65 each, valuing the company at £294 million. It announced its intention to expand annual output by 4,000 cars, equivalent to an 11 percent increase in output, and take on a further 530 workers across Britain. The share issue was heavily oversubscribed, and witnessed traffic jams and fights in the street as potential buyers struggled to enter their applications for stock. It was voted as one of the most successful share issues.

British Telecom

By far the largest floatation of a public corporation so far is that of the sale of 51 percent of the stock in British Telecom, for which the government realized some £4,000 million. Once again, a great deal of effort was put into ensuring that small investors played a part in the new company, and there were generous allocations for those applying for small numbers of shares, and for workers in the company. Vouchers, offering a discount on telephone bills, were available to individual shareholders who retained their holding for six months. A national TV and newspaper advertising campaign made the general public aware of the floatation and how to acquire shares.

The result was that when the shares were offered for sale in November 1984, they were oversubscribed by five times: over a million people applied for the shares. A number of the larger investing institutions were disappointed to find that they were allocated only around half of the shares they wanted to take up; members of the public were limited to a maximum of 800 shares, even if they had applied for more; and when trading started in early December, activity was brisk.

Although opponents of the transfer argued that the shares had been sold too cheaply, the wide involvement of the general public made it an undoubted success. Furthermore, careful conditions were put into the operating licence arrangements for Telecom which helped to counter opposition. These included conditions that the new company:

(a) would continue to provide a comprehensive telephone service where reasonable demand exists;

(b) would maintain emergency and rural telephone services; and

(c) would connect its system to competitors such as Mercury.

Conclusion

The Thatcher government has given considerable attention to preparing government-owned industries for privatization. Whether the sale is a whole enterprise, or separate parts of it, or of some of the shares in it, there are many government operations rendered unattractive to buyers by long years in the public sector. Bad business practices, depleted capital stock, feather-bedding at both management and labor levels, uneconomic working practices and poor production quality do not appeal to investors seeking high rates of return.

By subjecting bloated government enterprises to a strict regimen, however, the British government has brought many of them nearer to the point where they can become viable private sector operations. Managers have been appointed to bring about major changes by cutting down on loss-making activities and on feather-bedding practices. In some cases the removal of protective monopoly privileges has permitted competition to prompt similar moves. The overall result has been to increase the options for privatization through some form of sale.

METHOD FOUR: SELLING TO THE WORKFORCE

For some government activities it may be possible to sell the operation as a complete entity to the workforce. The obvious merit from the government's viewpoint is that this secures the co-operation of labor and management during the transition.

The reasoning behind this method points to the importance of motivation.

For most public sector activities, there is no strong link between employee performance and reward. Only recently in Britain have bonuses for increased productivity been used here and there as a major element in employee compensation. All too often there have been so-called 'incentive payments' whose real function has been to save face for a government forced to concede a higher wage increase than its current wage guidelines called for.

Workers who participate in the ownership of their company, on the other hand, have a real incentive to recognize their own interests within those of the firm. In employee-owned firms, restrictive practices stop and the quality of service leaps forward when the employees gain personally from reduced costs and increased sales. Workers are often in a good position to assess what effect on productivity and production would result if they become the owners of the firm. They can thus assess the viability of a privatized co-operative.

Just as the public expects better service from a manager who is also the owner, so it can expect better treatment from a firm whose workforce owns it. In this way the two large groups who are potential opponents of such a move — consumers and workers — both have their interests bound up in the change.

This is an appropriate method for privatizing the public sector when independent buyers might doubt their ability to achieve full-hearted co-operation from the employees under private management. The employees, as owners, know that they will do what is required. In this way it is possible for a loss to the government to be transformed into a profit for the workers, with the government receiving the proceeds of the sale in the bargain.

The National Freight Corporation

Britain's National Freight Corporation was sold to its employees, at their suggestion, and provides a remarkable case history of successful transfer.

The National Freight Corporation was established in Britain in 1969. It was done in an attempt to bring together under one roof all the road freight transport interests that the government had acquired. It was set up with an initial capital debt (excluding any payment of interest) of almost £100 million.

The government's plans for sale were outlined in a press notice of August 22, 1979. It was felt that National Freight's poor financial performance would prevent its sale by a straightforward flotation. In May 1981, a proposal for an employee buy-out was put to the government from within the NFC; and by October 1981 a conditional sale agreement had been signed. On February 19, 1982 the National Freight Company Ltd became a wholly-owned subsidiary of the National Freight Consortium — owned jointly by employees, pensioners of NFC and four banks.

The deficiency in NFC's pension schemes was to be funded by the government, and this had a considerable effect on the price which the government received. NFC was sold for £53.5 million but, after deducting the contribution to the pension funds and miscellaneous expenses incurred in the sale, the government made only about £6 million net.

The sale of the NFC to its employees has been a spectacular success. A company whose poor financial performance was felt to stand in the way of a sale has been transformed into a highly profitable enterprise. The first annual shareholders' meeting following privatization attracted considerable press attention. It transpired that the company had made good profits. Shareholder-employees thus had the double satisfaction of seeing their investment pay dividends, and of enjoying a considerable capital appreciation.

Their comments to the media were revealing. One summed it up by describing the new working conditions as a different world from that of employment by the state. Gone were the demarcation disputes, and in their place was a determination to get on with it and make a success. The NFC has continued to prosper, and is a major example of privatization via sale to the workforce. It provides a dramatic contrast with the highly-subsidized workers in the state sector.

Redhead

A second worker buy-out took place at the Redhead shipyard. In 1977 the British Labor government took over the main private shipyards and established British Shipbuilders as a state concern. Since that time it has continually faced one problem after another, with losses reaching £109.7 million in 1979. Despite an improvement in productivity of 15 percent between 1981 and 1982, and a reduction in the workforce from 86,700 when nationalized in 1977 to around 60,000 by 1982, it continued to make losses.

The British Shipbuilders Bill, first introduced in late 1982, was intended not to be a direct privatization attempt, but more of an enabling act giving the Secretary of State the necessary powers to direct the corporation to dispose of assets by forming and then selling subsidiary companies. British Shipbuilders comprised no less than nineteen shipbuilding companies, five companies involved in the manufacture of slow speed diesel marine engines, and three training companies.

The Minister of State for Industry in early 1983, Mr Norman Lamont, was obviously thinking of something like the Redhead shipyard when he said that he was looking for 'an opportunity to allow a breath of private capital and enterprise into the state-owned industry.'

The Redhead ship repair yard at South Shields was closed by the state-controlled British Shipbuilders in October 1982. Some eighty of the workers then came together, pooling their £110,000 lay-off payments, and bid for the yard. Within the state sector there were fears that the new operation might siphon work away from them. An impossible price of £300,000 was set, but this was reduced after the 1983 election, and the deal was closed.

The workers' group is paying off the purchase price over eight years at 4 percent above the prime interest rate. They have the option to complete the purchase at any time without the payment of further interest. The private yard opened in October 1983, with 22 of the 80 shareholders at work, seeking the orders that could put the rest of them to work. By January 1984, 110 men were at work, with the expectation that total employment would soon rise to 150.

As with the National Freight Corporation, the notorious inter-union disputes have vanished; and the new firm's brochure advertises a 'guarantee of no strikes, no overtime bans, no demarcation disputes, sensible flexibility, and minimum lost time.'

The Redhead move is not yet a success story, but is well on the way to becoming one as business picks up. It illustrates the value of the technique for even the most depressed and difficult industries. In a field of chronic labor disputes, it is revealing to hear the words of one of its founders, shop-floor director Jim Todd: 'It's a long time since I've heard singing and laughing in a shipyard.'

Victualic

The plastics firm Victualic was another successful buyout. In early 1983, British Steel sold Victualic, a firm making plastic pipes and joints, and rubber gaskets and seals, to its workforce. Out of a total of 885 workers, 634 put up a total of £838,000 for a 40 percent share in the company — British Steel retains 30 percent with Barclays Bank and various others holding the balance. The average holding is £400 per worker, but some spent as much as £5,000 on buying a share in their company.

The exercise appears to be succeeding beyond anyone's dreams. In fact, each share bought for £1 in 1983 is now valued at £1.98, meaning that each worker who bought shares has effectively doubled his money.

METHOD FIVE: GIVING TO THE PUBLIC

There may be elements of the public sector where a sale is inappropriate, but where an outright gift can be made. For firms which have experienced large losses over the years, it would be more accurate to talk of disposing of public liabilities than of handing out state assets. Since the public sector is already technically in 'public ownership,' the only difference made by a gift to the general public is that people receive an assigned and specific share, instead of having a notional claim on the whole. But this makes a big difference because once their share is identified it becomes alienable, meaning it can be sold or otherwise disposed of.

It may be feasible, for certain public operations, to distribute to the general public the shares which they already own notionally. In some cases those who worked in the industry might be given additional shares, but the expectation in either case would be that shareholders would be represented eventually by a management group with plans for turning a profit through re-organization. After a period of time one would expect to see a company operating as part of the private sector, albeit with a very diversified ownership.

This is similar in many respects to the method used to dispose of the Volkswagen company after the World War II. Its obvious advantage is that it ends public liability, while restoring the operation to the private sector. In cases where everyone receives their piece of the company, the acquiescence of the general public is gained. Workers in the company might face an increased risk to their jobs, so it may be advisable to grant them additional shares to put them high on the list of the direct beneficiaries from any improvement in productivity.

In cases where specific individuals receive benefits from a costly public sector activity, the beneficiary group can be counted on to oppose the distribution of the 'assets' if a loss of their benefit results. It might be appropriate in such cases to make the beneficiary group the recipients of the gift, to counter the loss which would otherwise be incurred.

There is still no clear-cut example of the British government actually giving away to the general public a 'publicly' owned asset in its entirety. There are numerous examples of some shares being given to workforces or the public who buy shares in a firm — usually on a one-to-one basis with the purchaser getting a certain number of free shares on the condition that he buys some of his own.

One minor example of a gift to the public is worthy of note because it represents a break from the more conventional privatization methods. It concerns the sale of British Telecom. Because of the size of the sale — most estimates suggest a value of £4 billion — there was fear that it would swamp the market and not achieve its 'true' value. So, in order to encourage far wider share ownership, and overcome the problems that might occur with such a large sale, the government went ahead with a voucher incentive scheme whereby those buying BT shares received a discount on their telephone bill. This took the form of giving individual investors vouchers of a fixed amount which can be offset against their quarterly telephone bills over a limited period ahead. The number and value of the vouchers received by an investor was related to the amount invested at the time of flotation and held over the period, subject to a maximum.

Cases of whole industries being given to the public have not occurred yet, although this has been suggested by many Conservative thinkers, as well as by Dr David Owen, leader of the Social Democratic Party.

METHOD SIX: GIVING TO THE WORKFORCE

There may be areas of state supply suitable for transformation into worker co-operatives by an outright gift to the employees, together with the writing off of any capital debt. This treatment is suggested for operations in which a history of public subsidy points to the need for major reorganization, and the possibility of sale to the workforce is unlikely.

There are undoubtedly some areas of the public sector where the industrial power of the workforce and the history of labor relations are sufficiently discouraging to outweigh the value of capital, land, stock, equipment and other assets. To anyone except the workforce, the operation might have a negative value and pose the prospect of a continual drain on future resources. For the workforce, however, the prospect might be viewed quite differently. Working for themselves in a co-operative might lead them to change their attitudes and work habits more than any management from outside could. The workers' own leaders might be quite different if they were elected on some basis other than their ability to drive tough bargains with government. As with several of the other methods of dealing with public sector problems, this one takes advantage of the propensity of workers to do better when they work for themselves than when they work for others.

In practice, such a form of transfer could take place only with the full agreement of the workforce. The employees might well prefer the prospect of remaining public employees, confident of their power to exact continuous subsidies and to achieve better rewards for themselves at the expense of the rest of society. Only if there were serious prospects of that state of affairs not continuing will there be any incentive for serious consideration of a workers' co-operative. Part of the price which government might have to pay is the continuation of certain subsidies which are withdrawn on a gradual basis over several years, as the new co-operative grows. By continuing subsidies on a short-term basis, government might find itself with a solution to even the most intractable loss-making areas of the public sector.

There is obviously a limited number of cases in which this method of privatization is appropriate. One factor to be considered would be the possibility of placing an essential service entirely in the hands of a militant union (insofar as it is not already in such hands). Another would be the desire to avoid substituting a private monopoly for a public one.

Hovercraft services

There is a case history in Britain of a public sector enterprise being given over to its workforce. This was done with the English Channel hovercraft ferry service formerly owned by British Rail, the state railroad service, in association with a Swedish firm as a result of a previous merger.

In mid-February 1984, British Rail sold its 50 percent share interest in Hoverspeed for a nominal sum of £1 to a staff consortium, with the co-owners doing likewise. Thus Hoverspeed was given away to its management and workforce, and is now wholly owned within the private sector.

METHOD SEVEN: CHARGING FOR THE SERVICE

Charging prices for public services is a variety of partial privatization. Just as the production of goods and services may be in the public or in the private sector, the *finance* of production also may be in either sector. Charging prices for public services involves taking the finance into the private sector, while leaving the production in the public sector.

The reasoning behind this tactic is that a system of direct pricing can bring some economic disciplines to bear where there were none before. For goods or services which are 'free' — that is, financed out of general taxation — the demand is potentially infinite. It is in everyone's interest to consume individually as much as possible of goods which are paid for collectively. In practice this involves considerable economic dislocation, with all kinds of services hopelessly oversubscribed and rationed either by waiting lists or by political influence.

The switch to finance through consumer charges immediately inhibits frivolous demand, and directs funds to those areas where real value for consumers is demonstrated. It tends to limit over-production and over-supply, and to act as a restraining influence on costs.

There are some operational difficulties to taking the finance of public services into the private sector by means of charging for services. While some areas, notably the public utilities in Britain, have long featured direct charges, there has always been public resistance to price increases, and such increases have always been politically sensitive. Where charges have not been traditional, there is considerable resentment to their imposition by recipients of the 'free' service. These recipients enjoy a good deal of media sympathy, accompanied by graphic portrayal of real or apparent hardship caused by the charging of prices.

Where successfully introduced, the practice of charging prices puts pressure on legislators to support uneconomically low prices, and to maintain artificially low prices by means of subsidies. The general taxpayers are insufficiently organized or visible to counter these pressures. Every year, legislators risk unpopularity if they keep the charges at a level which reflects true costs. Therefore, charging prices cannot be part of a permanent movement from public to private sector, but it is certainly better than having both production *and* finance in the public domain. Its best use is perhaps in limited areas as a step toward a fuller transfer and as a means of bringing in the economic disciplines which will make complete privatization possible later.

Examples

Britain's National Health Service provides case histories. Charges for spectacles, dentistry and prescriptions serve to illustrate its application.

Charges for prescriptions over recent years have been:

1973	20p
1979	45p
1980	70p and later £1.00
1982	£1.30
1983	£1.40

Income generated from these represents:

1978-79	£24.4 million
1979-80	£38.9 million
1980-81	£71.2 million
1981-82	£87.2 million
1982-83	£105 million

Nevertheless, the charge is a small fraction of the cost of many prescriptions, and political pressures have led to exemptions being granted to certain groups. There are many exemptions but the main groups are women beyond retirement age, children under 16, pregnant women and those who gave birth during the last 12 months, people receiving Family Income Supplement or supplementary benefit, those suffering from certain medical disorders. The effect is to confine payments to those who can afford them.

Dental and optical charges were first introduced in 1951, and currently there is a maximum charge for routine dental treatment of £13.50, while the most that can be charged for all forms of treatment is £95. For spectacles the maximum charge is £30, though most are less than this. All check-ups are free. At the moment there are no charges for, the examination of teeth, the arrest of bleeding, repairs to dentures, and essential home visits. The government attempted to introduce a £2.00 fee for eye tests but dropped the idea.

The exemption groups are the same as for prescription charges. Government policy is to make charges increase in line with costs.

There are also charges for other items supplied by the National Health Service including elastic hosiery, surgical brassiere, abdominal or spinal supports, and certain wigs.

METHOD EIGHT: CONTRACTING OUT THE SERVICE TO PRIVATE BUSINESS

A further method of partial privatization involves keeping the finance in the public sector, but moving production over to the private economy. Instead of using in-house direct labor to produce goods and services, independent businesses are paid from public funds to perform the task. Successful changeover to contract services involves inviting competitive tenders from companies seeking the work.

This method involves a recognition that government can still be responsible for guaranteeing a supply, even when it does not produce that supply itself. The immediate advantage to government and taxpayers is the savings, normally in the 20-40 percent range. The public usually gains an improved, more up-to-date service. The workforce is usually reduced, because private firms use labor more efficiently.

Resistance by unions and employees is weakened by the fact that private businesses often give workers better opportunities and incentives. In Britain private pension benefits tend to be lower than price-indexed government pensions, but basic pay, bonuses and other fringe benefits are often as good as or better than their state counterparts. The unions, which stand to lose public sector powers of leverage, are the main groups opposed to the use of contractors. In Britain they have spent millions, unsuccessfully, in an attempt to curtail contracting out.

An intelligent use of private business under contract normally will specify that the successful bidder give preferential treatment to existing employees before taking on new labor. It will involve pre-selection of bidders, so that only businesses known to be reputable and stable will be involved in the performance of essential work. It will involve penalty clauses for non-delivery of service, often with bonds being lodged to guarantee payment. Every effort needs to be made to placate possible sources of anxiety about whether private business will be sufficiently reliable. The above measures, together with careful specification of tasks in the contract, will allay such worries.

The general advantages are enormous. With production in the private sector, economic disciplines are introduced. An entire history of restrictive practices and labor-controlled services is wiped out overnight and replaced by a competitive climate. But attempting to win and retain the contract, firms are kept competitive in price and quality. Costs go down because men and machinery are used efficiently.

If it chooses government can seek to cover some of the costs of terminating the service by selling capital equipment to the new private supplier. In this way the initial costs of lay-off pay to discharged employees can be covered.

The use of private contractors on a growing scale to perform local government services in Britain, provides a whole range of case histories. It has been an astonishing success, and continues to gain momentum.

Local government services

Even though the private sector handles 98 percent of all hazardous waste disposal in Britain it is surprising that no major local refuse service was put out for bid until 1980. In that year, Southend-on-Sea invited tenders for the provision of garbage collection, street sweeping and lavatory maintenance. Of the six bids submitted, the winning offer by Exclusive Cleansing and Exclusive Cleaning led to a total savings of £492,000.

The overwhelming success of this venture led to a trickle of local authorities following Southend's example. This trickle turned into a flood as the cost-saving and improved service became more apparent. The flood has now turned into a torrent with hardly a day going by without one more local authority privatizing another part of its services.

Statistical information has tended to underestimate significantly the number of local authorities who contract out their services, since few records are kept centrally. Nevertheless, information provided through surveys by independent organizations indicates how explosive the growth has been.

In October 1983, *Public Service Review* provided a list of thirty-one different authorities who had privatized a service. By December 1983 this had increased to forty-six authorities and rose to fifty-five by March 1984. Not only is this figure expected to continue to rise, but the phenomenon of cities contracting out more than one service, once they see the advantages it brings, is also expected to increase.

The government has also introduced and extended certain measures of compulsory bidding, mostly for local authority construction and maintenance work. Currently, all maintenance work which costs above £10,000, and 30 percent of the work costing less than £10,000 has to be put out to bid. In addition, any new building work costing more than £50,000 plus one-third of less expensive work has to be put out for bid. There are motions in the pipeline to introduce compulsory tendering for 60 percent of the new building work *below* the £50,000 threshold. These reforms have enabled private contractors to carry out more than half of the local authority work on highways, construction and general maintenance. Public sector workforces carry out 61.2 percent of general maintenance, 53 percent of highway work, and between 16 percent and 24.4 percent in construction.

Such a huge range of services have been successfully privatized that each week now sees the privatization of yet more services somewhere by more local authorities. The policy has meant immense savings to taxpayers nationwide.

Table 2
Local government services contracted out to private industry

Local authority	Operation	Annual savings
Bath City	public lavatory & street cleaning & refuse collection	£300,000
	catering in council & sports halls	£63,000
Birmingham City	school cleaning	£640,000
Boothferry	pest control	£14,390
Bromley	street cleaning	£200,000
Broxbourne	public convenience cleaning	£11,000
Cambridgeshire	school cleaning	£700,000
Chiltern	refuse collection	£160,000
Christchurch	public convenience cleaning	£16,000
Croydon	public convenience cleaning	£70,000
	pest control	£20,000
Dover	public convenience cleaning	*

Table 2 (continued)

Local authority	Operation	Annual savings
Dudley	school cleaning	£600,000
	further education college cleaning	£130,000
Ealing	street cleaning	£600,000
	school meals	£695,000
	meals on wheels	
East Staffs	electrical contractors	£3,000
Eastbourne	street cleaning	£500,000
	refuse collection	
Edinburgh	architectural services	*
Epping Forest	pest control	£2,000
	delivery/collection of polling equipment	£365
	vending service	£7,000
Fareham	public convenience cleaning	£22,000
Gedling	office cleaning	£12,000
Gillingham	public convenience cleaning	£30,350
Gloucester	horticultural produce	£24,000
Gt Yarmouth	office cleaning	£6,114
Humberside	meals on wheels	£43,000
The Royal Borough of Kensington & Chelsea	refuse collection	£14,000
Kent	school cleaning	£1,100,000
Kingston	grass cutting	£46,000
Lewes	public convenience cleaning	£7,000
Lothian	car parks leased	£155,000
Maldon	street cleaning	£1,180
Mendip	refuse collection	£126,000
Merton	school meals	£750,000
	school cleaning	£250,000
	refuse and waste paper collection	£750,000
Milton Keynes	refuse collection	£488,000
North Norfolk	refuse collection	£175,000
Penwith	public convenience cleaning	£30,000
St Albans	public convenience cleaning	£20,000

Table 2 (continued)

Local authority	Operation	Annual savings
St Edmundsbury	golf course leased	£15,000
Salisbury	pest control	£12,000
South Bucks	pest control	£7,000
	office cleaning	£2,000
South Lakeland	grass cutting	£1,500
South Oxfordshire	refuse collection	£200,000
Southend-on-Sea	street cleaning	£600,000
	refuse collection	
Surrey Heath	street cleaning	£12,000
Sutton	cleaning of libraries	£3,500
	laundry	£14,000
Tamworth	refuse collection	£200,000
Tandridge	refuse collection	£160,000
Taunton Dene	refuse collection	£42,700
Vale of White Horse	street cleaning & refuse collection	£290,000
Wandsworth	street cleaning	£670,000
	refuse collection	£1,130,000
Waverley	golf course leased	£2,000
City of Westminster	architectural services	£235,000
Wirral	street cleaning & refuse collection	£1,400,000
Wycombe	office cleaning	£3,455
Yeovil	office cleaning	£21,500

*Authority unwilling to give figures
Source: *Public Service Review* No. 3, 1984.

Hospital ancillary services

The use of contractors in the National Health Service is not entirely new. But the recent expansion in contracting, especially for catering and cleaning in hospitals, is new.

In previous years the use of contractors has been handicapped, not only because there was no obligation to go out to tender, but also because of an asymmetric policy on

Value Added Tax. A health authority employing direct labor would not have to pay VAT, but if outside contractors were used, VAT had to be charged. Despite this, out of the ninety area health authorities in England in 1981-82, many contractors were good enough to overcome the tax burden, and win contracts in twenty-four authorities to provide catering services, and in eighty-eight authorities to provide domestic cleaning services. The total value of these, including laundry was over £17 million.

The savings by taking private business bids to perform services can be both direct and indirect. On the one hand, if the private contractor is better and cheaper, the costs are lowered. On the other hand, even if the service is still retained in-house, then the mere threat of competition can produce savings. Any savings on a bill of almost £800 million per year will be reallocated into additional patient care and medical equipment.

In a recent Health Ministry circular the government asked health authorities to test the cost of their support services in order to discover whether savings can be made and resources released for improved patient services. It also tackled the tax problem, and made arrangements for this VAT to be refunded to health authorities from September 1, 1983.

Privatizing the services of health authorities includes more than domestic, catering, and laundry services. For example, Southern Derbyshire Health Authority is considering estimated savings of £24,000 a year by closing down four oil-powered boilers and buying steam from a private contractor. Certain regional health authorities contract out their abortion services to private agencies. Private firms are being used in Somerset to take surgical waste to incineration, and many health authorities are either renting mobile operating theatres or are sending patients to private hospitals, in a successful attempt to reduce waiting lists.

Meals at British schools

Most local authorities provide lunch for British schoolchildren, and most do so by employing their own labor. In view of the high cost of this, it is not surprising that some education authorities have attempted to obtain the advantages of privatizing their school meal service. It was the London Borough of Merton which made the first move, and the service is now provided by Sutcliffe Catering Company (South) Ltd, who started preparing 6,500 meals a day from September 5, 1983. The general reception to the change was summed up by a local headmaster, Mr Hugh Streeter who said: 'We are delighted. The meals are presented on very colorful and attractive trays and the children love them.'

Innovation by private firms, such as the provision of vending machines at Hillcrest School in Dudley (W Midlands), is an obvious advantage that keeps the children happy, and at the same time saves money. But as with most local contracting out, however, there are problems of calculating how extensive the privatization program is. Nevertheless, indications are that the success of Merton is duplicated elsewhere. In January 1984, East Sussex County Council announced that it is inviting tenders for the provision of meals in its forty schools, and Hereford set up an innovative workers' co-operative scheme.

Whatever the result, one thing is sure. The provision of school meals by private contractors is expanding.

Other examples of contracting out

(1) Testing of trucks and public vehicles. The 1982 British Transport Act allowed for the annual testing of heavy goods vehicles and public service vehicles to be transferred to the private sector.

(2) British Telecom — coin collection. British Telecom has contracted out coin collection from public payphones to Pritchard Security Ltd for an undisclosed sum.

(3) Pollution emergencies. The British Defense Department and the Transport Department have transferred the task of maintaining and storing emergency cargo transfer equipment to the private sector. Specialized equipment for dealing with pollution emergencies is now stored centrally and maintained by United Towing Ltd.

(4) Government buildings and maintenance. Of the many thousands of construction contracts and design commissions that the Property Services Agency handles each year, it has become policy that all new construction and over 80 percent of maintenance work is carried out by private contractors. In 1982-83, 42 percent of project design was done by private consultants.

(5) Grass cutting in Northern Ireland. In 1981 the Northern Ireland Housing Executive contracted out the cutting of grass.

(6) Health authorities — auditing. By November 1983, nine firms of accountants held contracts to undertake audits of fourteen district health authorities previously audited by staff at the British Health Ministry.

(7) Road construction units. By 1981, the road construction units (which design roads and freeways in Britain) had handed over to private consultants virtually all of their work, amounting to projects worth approximately £2,000 million.

(8) Civil Service — catering. Mr Barney Hayhoe, the Civil Service Minister, announced in December 1983 that more than half of the 654 Civil Service Restaurants and cafeterias have in recent years been operated by private contractors.

(9) Ministry of Defense cleaning. There are some 920 defense and armed forces units in Britain. Of these, 672 are currently cleaned by private contractors and a further 72 have signed contracts for the future.

(10) Southern Electricity Board — cash security. Pritchard Securities won the bid from Britain's Southern Electricity Board for what it says is its biggest cash-handling security service. The exact value has yet to be disclosed, but the work covers the collection of cash and checks, and wage distribution for the Board's 120 shops and offices from Yeovil and Cirencester to Bognor Regis and the Isle of Wight.

(11) British Steel — contract labor. Initial Services has supplied British Steel with contract labor for twenty years, including new plant and ingot dressing services, where the Initial men burn the impurities off the steel which is produced.

(12) Central Office of Information — film unit. From April 1, 1982, the work of the Central Office of Information film unit was transferred to private film-makers.

(13) British National Bus Company. In the National Bus Company report of 1982 it says that NBC contracted out catering, building repairs and cleaning, tire maintenance, and cash security services. The hire of other operators' vehicles to enable the company to meet peak commitments amounted to 5.6 million miles of operations in 1982.

(14) British government departments. All government departments in Britain use private firms in one way or another. The most common form of contracting out appears to be for private security firms to safeguard buildings and transport of valuable or potentially dangerous items. However, other examples include cleaning, training, catering, construction work, maintenance, architectural work, surveying and even the deck chair service in royal parks.

(15) Post Office — parcel mail. The Post Office invited tenders for the delivery of parcel mail to Paris for a year beginning in the summer of 1984.

(16) British Rail — miscellaneous experiments. There are a total of seventy private franchises operating in British Rail stations, and while there has been delay in privatizing some on-train catering, experiments with private companies providing minor on-train services has begun.

(17) Servicing of ships and aircraft. The British Ministry of Defense is currently handing over the major servicing of Royal Navy ships and Royal Air Force front-line aircraft to private contractors.

(18) Army laundering. With the exception of the British Army on the Rhine and in the Falklands, all laundering for the Army is contracted out. The contract is worth approximately £3.5 million per year.

(19) Prison services. Most of the work concerned with the design and construction of prisons is performed privately, as well as the domestic catering and night security services at two staff training establishments.

(20) Arms trials overseas. The Ministry of Defense is currently organizing the contracting out of support activities for overseas trials undertaken by the AAEE (Aeroplane and Armament Experimental Establishments).

METHOD NINE: DILUTING THE PUBLIC SECTOR

For parts of the public sector where there is no possibility of moving existing operations toward the private sector, it may be possible to have maintenance and expansions done privately.

The effect is to lower the proportion of work done by the public sector without changing the availability of the service to the public.

Chronic capital shortage is a standing weakness of the public economy. At all times, and especially in recession, extension of a network of services presents a problem. One solution is to find ways of bringing private enterprise in to do the task. The injection of private capital into the work of restoration and expansion of the public network can take the pressure off the public purse, bringing the much needed improvement in service without further burdens on the taxpayer.

Private capital always seeks a positive return, and intricate devices are sometimes required to establish genuine risk-capital ventures in the public sector. If private firms put up the money and perform the work for a guaranteed return from government, this is simply public sector borrowing by another name, and fails to take the pressure off public spending. What is required is a means of allowing private entrepreneurs to take risks based on the anticipated use of the new or rebuilt parts of the network.

When risk is built into the system, two important results emerge. The first is that the private funding is then not regarded as public sector borrowing, but private investment. The other result is that only those parts of the public network which are most certain of a demand will be renewed or extended. The introduction of risk, in other words, serves to direct private funds to where the need is greatest. Whether the public network involves roads, water facilities or other types of public systems, the private capital to develop or renew public facilities has to seek its returns through customer use. In this way the money will be attracted to where entrepreneurs think it will most likely serve an unsatisfied need.

The attraction for legislators of bringing private capital to the aid of a traditionally public network is that it enables work to be done with a minimum of public outlay. It is often noted how infrastructures suffer when there is a squeeze on public money. With this type of approach, however, an infrastructure can be maintained and extended without massive outlays of public funding. The repayment is made over the years according to use.

Private building, engineering and contracting firms are natural allies of government in the introduction of such schemes. The employees of these companies welcome the extra jobs which the work brings, and the public gains the benefit of the new or improved service. As the attractions of using this method spread, more and more renovation and extension projects will be done in the private sector. The size of the public sector thus will diminish without direct cuts in public funds or jobs. The effect is to dilute the proportion of a service which is done in the public sector.

Private road funding

Britain has recently developed road construction schemes which use private capital on a risk basis. Privately-funded road projects give an example of how work by the private sector can dilute the public holding even though the public service is still maintained.

When appointed by the British government to investigate potential road construction employing private capital, Charterhouse Japhet suggested the 'Black Country Road' near Wolverhampton. The plan has been top priority on the county council structure plan for two years, with the intention that an access road to the industrial area (mostly an eleven mile long area west and north-west of Birmingham) would help unemployment, which averaged 19 percent, but went as high as 30 percent in certain areas.

A consortium of National Westminster Bank, Tarmac Construction and Saturn Management, (known as TNS) became involved during Easter 1983. The Federation of Civil Engineering Contractors became interested and eventually started lobbying for it. 'The basis of the proposals is that TNS will provide a road to the design and specification of West Midlands County Council who will make payments based on actual traffic flows and actual commercial and industrial space developed within a specified area. These payments will commence when the road is open to traffic and cease twenty-five years later,' said the West Midlands submission to the Transport Department.

It was the prospect of the road being privately funded that offered hope for the project to proceed in a fast, flexible and efficient manner. When coupled with the competitive tendering procedures adopted for actual construction work, this could mean that the road might be completed in five years. State funding, the Council estimated, would make it unlikely for the road to be finished in less than ten or twelve years. The reason is that state funding for the project would be divided into two stages: interim funding for the construction period and long-term funding for the operating period. By having private funding, total finance would be in place before construction starts, while state funding would be on a yearly basis and would lack both certainty and security.

The British Department of Transport rejected the first proposal, on economic grounds, after long consideration. Meanwhile, the West Midland County Council is going ahead using state funds (via the Transport Supplementary Grant) to start construction. Other privately-funded plans are under consideration.

Development of housing

With Britain's local authorities having to reconsider expenditure commitments over the last few years, privatization has become a high priority. The year 1983 saw the introduction of the private development of public housing projects in Britain. In Priesthill, one of Glasgow's problem areas of low-quality housing, Barratt (the housebuilding firm) is taking over 190 council houses. It will upgrade and sell them. In the case of Priesthill, they will be on offer for £18,000 for a two bedroom unit. Other councils, such as in Liverpool, are adopting the idea.

The idea appears to have greatest appeal in areas where there are large numbers of poor-quality government-owned houses, and where the authority concerned has little or no money to carry out the necessary improvements. The net result is that local authorities can improve the quality of housing within their area at no extra cost. The much-needed repair of housing goes ahead, and the tenants even get the opportunity to buy the house after redevelopment.

National Bus Company

The National Bus Company welcomed the possibility of

involving private capital in improving facilities, and as a result set up National Bus Properties Ltd. They also became involved in joint ventures with the private sector in express and coach holiday business.

British Steel Corporation

British Steel has been involved in what are known as the 'Phoenix' companies. The first was Phoenix I, set up by British Steel with the private firm of Guest, Keen and Nettlefold in February 1981. It traded independently under the name Allied Steel and Wire Ltd. Phoenix II was to have been a subsequent joint operation between BSC and the private sector, this time in the engineering steels sector. The venture remains stalled in negotiations.

High-tech industrial parks

High-tech industrial parks are attempts to bring together state-run universities and private industry to a common location — usually involving well laid-out industrial areas near universities or polytechnic institutes — to develop formal and informal links between private business and the state higher education establishment. The first park opened at Cambridge in 1970. Since 1979 a total of ten parks have been established, two are awaiting to be announced, and a further eighteen sites were being considered.

METHOD TEN: BUYING OUT EXISTING INTEREST GROUPS

When existing special interests have the power to thwart a move to the private sector, it may be possible to use a technique which alters the pattern for the future, even while continuing to benefit the present beneficiaries. In this way the service can be phased into the private sector over a period of years, and without threat to existing interests.

For example, proposals to abolish rent control and restore a private market in rental property seem unable to make headway in the face of opposition from those who live in artificially low-priced housing and their supporters. Proposals to end rent controls for *new* properties and *new* leases, however, will not face the same level of opposition because they allow existing tenants to continue to enjoy their subsidies. Such proposals in a sense 'buy out' the present generation in order to phase in a new system.

There are parts of the public sector in which long-term commitments have been entered into, and where benefits have long been enjoyed. In some of these areas the beneficiary group forms a identifiable and politically active group, ready to defend its privilege. Clearly there is a case for continuing to honor existing commitments while shutting off the route whereby new beneficiaries can enter the system. The present generation has its opposition allayed by the continuation of its benefits. Yet, this group forms a diminishing band if their numbers are not renewed.

This method sets in motion a chain of events whose process gradually but inexorably diminishes the publicly-controlled supply, and gradually enhances the proportion covered by the private market. It culminates in the extinction of what may seem another intractable part of the public sector.

Shorthold tenancies

The Thatcher government's introduction of new short-term tenancies and assured tenancies serves as an example of the technique of withdrawing public sector participation for newcomers into a system, while allowing those already within the system to continue in the benefits they receive from it.

The 'Protected Shorthold Tenancy' is a form of renting between private landlords and their tenants. It is designed to deal with some of the problems generated by rent control in Britain. It was brought into effect in November, 1980, under the British Housing Act. The main feature of the shorthold lease is that it allows landlords to rent property for a period between one and five years, while retaining the right of repossession at the end of the tenancy.

There are certain safeguards for tenants, and other requirements, before a letting can qualify as a shorthold. The lease must be to a new tenant, tenants have security of tenure during the period of the tenancy, the landlord must give due notice both to prospective tenants when a shorthold is being offered, and to the sitting tenant of his intention to repossess the property, and for all shortholds outside Greater London before December 1, 1981 and for all shortholds per se in the Greater London area after November 28, the dwelling must be registered for a fair rent with a Rent Officer.

Assured tenancies

The same Act created the 'Assured Tenancy' scheme. This permits recently-built homes in England and Wales to be excluded from the Rent Acts. In many ways it is similar to the shorthold tenancy scheme, in that the landlord has to give notice of the end of the tenancy, unless the tenant breaks one of the conditions of the tenancy. A significant difference is that the assured tenant can apply to the local authority for a new tenancy, whereas no such right exists with a shorthold.

To qualify the landlord must be an approved body, construction of the building must have started on or after August 8, 1980 (even extensively altered property since that day cannot qualify), and if previously rented, it must only have been an assured tenancy.

Therefore, the scheme is for newly-built properties, and by exempting them from the Rent Act, it allows the establishment of a freely negotiated market rent.

In November 1983, a government spokesman announced that there were 121 bodies approved under the assured tenancy scheme, representing a 300 percent increase since November 1982. Estimates of the number of homes they intended to provide are in the process of being re-assessed upwards, as the number of approved bodies has risen significantly.

METHOD ELEVEN: SETTING UP COUNTER GROUPS

Many of the ways which make it possible to have state-provided goods and services transferred to the private economy involve assuring interest groups that they will not lose in the process. Their potential opposition is neutralized if they stand to gain from the move. However, it is not always possible to ensure that every single interest group will benefit. Indeed, there are some groups which enjoy wide power and privilege at public expense. If the general public is to benefit, it is sometimes necessary to transfer the powers and privileges from the few and distribute them to the many.

The task of scaling back the public economy, therefore, sometimes involves a careful balancing of interests to ensure that there are more who gain than lose from the process. One type of proposal involves the creation of new groups of vested interests to counter-balance those whose benefits are linked to public sector supply. If the bureaucrats who administered a public program are to lose their power and status, for example, it is important that a new class of private managers see their own future tied up in the new order of things. The new people act as a counter group to outweigh the old. Those who once administered public operations and enjoyed the power of controlling state assets are balanced by a new group of owners in the private sector. The new owners will not willingly surrender their acquisition, and will form a group whose interests are tied to the new reality. Similarly, individuals who enjoy the choice and variety which private sector operation often brings to the consumer will not willingly forego the new freedom in order to return to the take-it-or-leave-it approach of state monopoly. They thus form an effective group whose interest is clearly aligned with the continued success of private supply.

There are specific cases in which the forces keeping an activity within the state sector can gradually be countered by the creation of a new interest group which recognizes its own gain from going private. In such cases the element of gradualism becomes important. An overnight change would not allow time for the new group to perceive and appreciate benefits that are only potential future gains. Actual experience of the private sector and its benefits creates a self-conscious group aware of its gains and prepared to oppose their elimination.

The creation of counter groups normally takes time, and is more appropriate to cases where privatization can be introduced gradually. The success of privatization spreads and secures the allegiance of beneficiaries until there are enough enjoying its benefits to outweigh those who object to the systematic diminution of the state's role.

Counter groups were created in Britain by the sale of state housing to existing tenants. The new property-owners have proved to be a powerful group in support of the new reality.

Council house sales

The disposal of public housing in Britain into private hands provides a case history of establishing a counter group. The houses were offered for sale to the current tenants at discounts of up to 50 percent.

More public sector housing in Britain (a total of 589,000 units) was transferred to the private sector between 1979 and 1982 than in the whole of the period since 1945. Central to this has been the introduction of the 'Right to Buy.' This came as a result of the 1980 Housing Act and the 1980 Tenants Rights (Scotland) Act, which gave tenants of local authorities, new towns and non-charitable housing associations the right to buy the homes they live in. It also granted the right to a mortgage, and the right to 'a discount off the open market value of the home, between a minimum of 33 percent rising to a maximum of 50 percent, contingent on the time spent as a tenant.'

A recent survey indicated that the typical former tenant who buys his own home is significantly older than other buyers and more likely to live in Scotland, Northern Ireland, or the North of England. More importantly the survey by Nationwide Building Society showed that he is also relatively poorer than other house-buyers. However, if a tenant is unable to afford to buy outright, by paying £100 he can have the option (for two years) to buy at the price the home was originally valued at. If the tenant buys in that time, the £100 goes towards the price of the house, otherwise it is refunded in full. For those who are unable to buy at the full value of the house there is the option for shared ownership. A tenant can buy a long lease of a house or flat for only a proportion of the dwelling's value (for example 25 percent, 50 percent or 75 percent) and that becomes the proportion which the tenant then owns. The rest is owned by the landlord, e.g., the local authority, and on that part the tenant still pays rent.

Table 3
Right to buy: progress of applications
1980 to July 1, 1983

Requests recieved	860,000
Acceptances issued	804,400
Sales completed	526,380

Shared ownership is aimed at those whose income is not big enough to qualify for a large mortgage. It allows the home owner to partly own and to partly rent his home. Some local authorities will offer discounts, but this is at their discretion. It is not uncommon for shares to be worked out on the sale price of the house. The shared ownership scheme had £40 million allocated to it in April, 1983, through the Housing Corporation, and it has proved to be a runaway success with almost 2,700 buyers being granted help, with thousands more inquiring. Unfortunately, the funding ran out after only three months, owing to the success of the scheme, and unless more funding is given the Housing Corporation says there will be no shared ownership scheme next year.

Table 4
Public sector housing sales between April 1, 1979
and June 1983
(figures rounded to nearest 500)

	'Right to Buy'	All sales
England	313,000	513,700
Wales	28,500	33,600
Scotland	25,500	41,600
	367,000	589,000

The Housing and Building Control Act of 1984 extends the right to buy. Its main purpose is:

(a) to increase the maximum discount available under the right to buy from 50 percent for tenants of twenty or more years tenancy, to 60 percent for tenants of thirty or more years tenancy;

(b) to increase the Secretary of State's powers to assist tenants experiencing difficulties in exercising their right to buy; and

(c) to introduce the 'right to repair' for tenants.

Table 5
Receipts from house sales (£ million at 1980 prices)

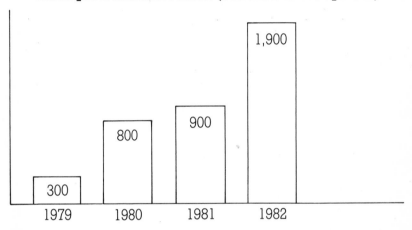

Source: *Lords Hansard,* V.446 c.916.

Private health care

Private health care in Britain also has generated a concrete counter group. The counter lobby is formed by the main 'provident' associations, which offer private health insurance and treatment, and have contributed greatly to the growth of health care in recent years.

The total membership of such schemes, including dependents, rose from 2.5 million in March 1979 to 4.2 million by the end of 1982. Many trade unionists are either members of the provident associations (some 350,000 are estimated to belong to the British United Provident Association), or of the Industrial Orthopaedic Society, which runs its own hospital, Manor House, in London.

Already the private sector cares for a number of National Health Service patients. In 1981-82 expenditure by health authorities on contractual arrangements with private hospitals and nursing homes for the care and treatment of National Health Service patients totalled £30.9 million, and 2,743 beds were occupied at the end of the year under such arrangements.

METHOD TWELVE: DEREGULATION VIA VOLUNTARY ASSOCIATIONS

Regulation might be thought of as an inherently governmental activity, but there are instances in which it can be effectively contracted out to voluntary associations. When state regulation is superseded by the self-regulation of a voluntary body, it marks a further retreat from the dominance of the public sector.

The advantages are manifold. Regulation by the state is a costly activity. It consumes the resources of both public and private sectors. It has a tendency to be performed insensitively, without regard to the costs of compliance. The bureaucrats who draw up and implement the regulations rarely have a detailed knowledge of the industry or activity with which they are concerned. Their edicts can have catastrophic consequences, especially on small firms operating on narrow margins.

Transferring the regulatory function to the private sector immediately reduces government costs and enables a reduction in the size of the public bureaucracy. While this is a bonus for taxpayers, the effect on the industry or activity concerned is more dramatic. A voluntary trade body or voluntary interest association consists of people who know the activity. They know how the costs of compliance fall upon those required to conform to the regulations, and generally can be counted on to come forward with more sympathetic and less costly ways of achieving the same results.

The switch to self-regulation by voluntary associations consulting with government creates a supportive group within the industry or activity which is regulated. There is also a potentially hostile element in the shape of lobby groups who learned to use the government agency to their own ends and who fear that the voluntary body will not be as co-operative. The important task here is to ensure the visible effectiveness of the new private bodies, and to secure the industry's agreement to those powers over their constituent members. In this way the general public can be satisfied that their interests are protected. They will not feel that industry is being allowed to pursue its interests at the expense of the public welfare.

Some areas of activity in Britain have long been subject to self-regulation. Bodies such as the Press Council have operated with a broad measure of public support and appreciation for their role. Case histories of a move away from governmental regulation toward the use of voluntary associations also are found in insurance and aviation. There has been a trend for government to phase-out many of its quangos — the quasi-autonomous organizations of the state — and rely instead on the expertise and advice of voluntary bodies.

Some examples

This device may be divided into two main areas: one involves shifting the burden of regulation from the state or state-appointed bodies towards private individuals or organizations. The other, being the more general of the two, involves measures taken to encourage the growth of voluntary effort.

Insurance and aviation. In the first instance, when regulation of the British insurance market was thought necessary following a series of scandals in 1982 with certain Lloyd's underwritings, the government passed the Lloyd's Act 1982 which set up a new ruling council to administer self-regulation.

Another example occurred after passage of the Civil Aviation Act in 1980. It abolished the government's powers of guidance over the industry and instead passed on the responsibility to the Civil Aviation Authority, to promote competition while maintaining the necessary regulation. At the moment this may represent only a decentralization of regulatory powers, but in the longer term there is the strong possibility that the CAA may be sold. Then the effort of the deregulatory guidance may be of greater significance.

Quangos. The abolition of a number of quangos (the quasi-autonomous state regulatory and advisory bodies), makes it clear that the function previously performed by the quango can be adequately done by a voluntary association. In January, 1982 Prime Minister Margaret Thatcher announced the abolition of quangos, three of which are of particular interest: The Advisory Committee on Bird Sanctuaries in the Royal Parks, The Advisory Committee on the Protection of Birds in England, and The Advisory Committee on the Protection of Birds in Scotland. No doubt central to their abolition was the view that they merely duplicated the activities of the Royal Society for the Protection of Birds (RSPB), an independent voluntary association.

Construction. The Housing and Building Control Bill provides another good example. It will encourage greater self-regulation by the construction industry, and at the same time simplify the building control system. The Bill's basic themes are the introduction of a less complicated and more flexible system of building regulations, and the introduction of private certification, whereby inspectors approved by the Secretary of State (or a designated body) will be able to supervise building work instead of the local authority.

Voluntary action. In 1948, Lord Beveridge produced a report entitled *Voluntary Action: A Report on Methods of Social Advance*, stressing his belief in voluntary effort — and this was from a man whom many regard as the father of the British welfare state. Voluntary effort is morally superior to state coercion; and since 1979 the Thatcher government has provided certain tax benefits to promote voluntary action. The major changes are reducing the minimum periods for tax-benefitted gifts from 7 to 4 years, removing the maximum limit (previously £100,000) on gifts to charities to be exempt from Capital Transfer Tax, and introducing tax relief for donors above the basic rate of tax.

METHOD THIRTEEN: ENCOURAGING ALTERNATIVE INSTITUTIONS

For a whole class of activities, the first step in the development of a trend toward private sector supply lies in demonstrating that there is a valid private alternative. Where public supply has dominated a field, informed opinion often questions the possibility of a valid private equivalent. This is hardly surprising. The informed opinion which makes its living in the public sector is securely entwined with the status quo and finds it difficult to conceive of alternatives.

It can be an important step in such cases to demonstrate that private operators can perform an equivalent service. The establishment of alternative institutions, which will serve to demonstrate that fact, is of prime importance. Since these are to be private bodies, the role of government in seeking movement toward the private sector should be one of encouragement.

Government can lend its goodwill toward private bodies set up in fields traditionally dominated by public supply. By doing so it allows them to prove their worth, and bring choice for the first time to the general public. In this way it fosters the growth of bodies which bring the merits of competition into the field. By encouraging alternative institutions to organize supply in a new way, government gives society access to innovative thinking and permits all kinds of new ideas to be tested, including ideas which may benefit the state sector of the activity.

The growth of institutions offering an alternative to the state supply offers not only a choice to consumers; it also takes away the state's role as sole employer in the field and brings forward the prospect of an alternative employer. The potential gain can be perceived by the general public as consumers, and by the employees of public sector firms.

The problem with alternative, private institutions is that, being private, they do not have the benefit of public finance or subsidy. Taxpayers who wish to acquire the services of these bodies will have to pay as consumers for a service they have already paid for as taxpayers. Despite this handicap, there are areas in which new private bodies can thrive in a field heavily dominated by the state. Government can assist them by encouragement. Instead of giving direct financial support, it can patronize them, consult them, and help to elevate their status and importance.

The success of new institutions of this nature lends powerful support to further moves toward privatization. Having seen that private alternatives can operate successfully, more experiments may be encouraged, with a gradually increasing role for private sector alternatives to state supply. When government wishes to make further moves toward private supply, the tried and tested alternatives point the way forward and, by this time, are accepted by the public as viable.

The University of Buckingham

The case history of Britain's University of Buckingham shows how encouragement by government has been able to help the development of a totally private alternative to the otherwise universal state university system. British Universities have long been organs of the state, supported by tax funds. The idea of a British University independent of government was first publicly aired on May 27, 1967, when *The Times* published a letter by Dr J W Paulley which contained the following statement:

'...is it not time therefore to examine the possibility of creating at least one new university in this country on the pattern of those great private foundations in the USA without whose stimulus and freedom of action the many excellent state universities in that country would be so much the poorer?'

No doubt this view seized the imagination of a large number of people, for by 1969 a signed declaration supporting the creation of an 'independent university' was published, and then in 1971, a site was found in Buckingham. Finally in 1976, Margaret Thatcher formally opened the College. Then on March 23, 1983, only seven years after opening, the Queen granted a Royal Charter, which established Buckingham as a full university.

The University has grown steadily over the years since its creation. In 1976 it had 65 students compared to 470 by early 1983. It intends to increase this figure to over 600 by the late 1980s. Financially it has improved, with a declared surplus of £28,696 in 1982, which it expects to increase in the immediate future. It has remained financially independent of the state.

The tuition fees for undergraduates in the 1984 academic year were £4,400 per annum. Students are eligible to receive mandatory awards from local authorities comprising a contribution to the above tuition fees (approximately one-third) and a maintenance grant.

Students can also obtain loans from the University's bankers toward the cost of tuition fees. Loans are repayable with interest over a maximum period of five years, commencing one month after completion of a student's course of studies. The bread and butter of the University is its law degree (LLB), but it also gives degrees in economics (BSc Econ), and the other arts and sciences.

The academic year comprises four ten-week terms, permitting students to complete an honors program in two calendar years, instead of the three years required at state institutions. This saves costs to the student — tuition, accommodation, etc. — and makes greater use of the resources of the University.

METHOD FOURTEEN: MAKING SMALL-SCALE TRIALS

Opposition to the withdrawal of government from an entire sector will be more muted if the undertaking is a limited and small-scale trial. The entire group of producers and consumers might be alarmed over large, sweeping moves to introduce into their area the disciplines of the private economy. A small-scale experiment, however, is not necessarily seen as a threat to the entire operation.

The experiment itself, if successful, serves to allay initial fears and prepares people for a more widespread extension of the principle. Possible disadvantages can be seen in the trial, and either prevented in subsequent applications, or they may serve as warnings against extension of the trial.

The public sector is characterized by conformity and standardized supply. Variation and choice, which are permitted and catered to by the private economy, are found rarely in the public sector. Thus, experimentation, which is continual in private enterprise, is not nearly as evident in the public sector. The use of experiments as a test of decontrol or deregulation within the public sector can be of crucial importance. The contrast between performance within the experiment and the results achieved by the state suppliers allows us to make judgements about government activities which cannot be gained by other means.

The use of experiments as a test of greater private sector involvement can be particularly effective as a way of establishing a principle. It is easier for people to endure a small test of privatization than to cope with a larger, more complete dose all at once. Added weight for the trial comes from locations which seek to gain the advantages which the experiment brings. An area seeking to attract industry and jobs might hope that its choice as an experimental site might encourage further development there.

When experimental trials are proposed, therefore, the opposition is divided by the potential gains and losses the trial will bring. National ideological opposition by one group can be balanced by enthusiastic lobbying for the venture by its local affiliates. A public sector union opposed to private inroads might find its own members eagerly seeking to be included in the pilot project.

The greatest merit of an experiment is that it minimizes the risk. If the project fails, the loss is confined to the test area. A success, on the other hand, can be extended area by area to other locations seeking similar benefits. In this way the domain of the private sector can be extended both gradually and safely.

Enterprise zones

The designation of enterprise zones in Britain as areas of selective deregulation serves as an example of the use of this technique. The pilot areas saw the removal of some of the impediments which restricted the development of new ventures.

Peter Hall, who originally conceived the idea of enterprise zones, had a very different concept from that which was finally adopted. He saw them much more as what would be regarded today as a deregulated freeport, free of UK taxation, social services, and regulations. There would be no (union) closed shop agreements, and the zones would be outside any exchange and customs controls.

In practice, Britain's enterprise zones differ from this concept in three main ways. Environmental and safety regulations remain in force, they do not have freeport status, and there is no deliberate encouragement to outside entrepreneurs to come in and establish *new* businesses in the zones.

What they do offer is a package of local incentives, with emphasis on seven points as follows.

(1) Exemption from local taxes on industrial and commercial property.
(2) Exemption from Development Land Tax.
(3) 100 percent write-off for Corporation and Income Tax purposes of capital expenditure on industrial and commercial buildings.
(4) Simplification of planning procedures and speedier administration of zoning controls for building and alterations.
(5) Reduction to a minimum of Government requests for statistical information.
(6) Employers exempt from charges for industrial training, and from requirement to supply information to Industrial Training Boards.
(7) Applications for customs facilities to be processed as a matter of priority.

British enterprise zones have in fact been used as yet another device for government assistance to economically depressed areas. Of the eleven zones originally designated, five were sited near areas where steel plants had closed, and seven were placed in economically assisted areas.

It cannot be said that enterprise zones represent free enterprise unhelped by government. According to one September 1983 estimate in *Public Money*, the 'local authorities and other government agencies spent an average of £7,000 per hectare on servicing and infrastructure' and that was in the first year alone. Areas designated as enterprise zones continue to be eligible for aid under the other government programs, such as the urban program and derelict land grant. It is also true, contrary to popular impressions, that local authorities and other public agencies retain a significant degree of control over the type and character of developments.

It is clear that the early effect of enterprise zone status was to increase significantly the level of economic activity in the zones. It is also clear that the cost of creating the estimated 2,900 jobs has not been cheap. There was an initial subsidy of £500,000 to firms moving in, and capital allowances amounting to £17.2 million — equal to £6,000 per new job. This does not include the cost of subsidizing those firms that were already there, estimated at millions worth of subsidies, and some £41.6 million invested in off-site works and factory construction. This illustrates the point that the end result was not unbridled capitalism.

Exactly what the original eleven enterprise zones achieved and whether they were successful has been the subject of much debate. What is clear is that the enterprise zones in practice bear little comparison to Peter Hall's original idea. The zones have been criticized for not going far enough and for being still too restrictive on enterprise.

The government obviously believes the enterprise zones are worthwhile because, after designating the first eleven between June 1981 and April 1982, Chancellor of the Exchequer Sir Geoffrey Howe outlined thirteen other sites on July 27, 1982.

Freeports

In 1983, the Thatcher government announced that it intended to set up a limited number of experimental freeports. This followed an initiative from the Adam Smith Institute.

Similar to the US foreign trade zones, the freeports were intended to give certain advantages to firms which located within them. Benefits included:

(a) simplification of customs procedures, leading to savings in costs for traders, and swifter turn-around of imported and exported goods;

(b) a cash flow benefit to zone users from not having to pay duty until goods were brought into the country;

(c) a ring fence and customs control on freeports offering to traders a secure environment which should be reflected in lower insurance costs;

(d) economies of scale achieved from the physical concentration of facilities;

(e) locations dedicated to international trade and likely to act as exhibition centres;

(f) international marketing of freeports as locations with particular appeal to overseas companies seeking an offshore bridgehead to the European market; and

(g) the relative absence of customs formalities, calculated to attract small firms which might be unaware of, or unable to cope with, the formalities involved in existing facilities for goods designed for re-export.

Some of these benefits are already available under existing custom procedures.

Six freeports were designated on February 2, 1984, chosen from 41 applications. The successful ones are listed in Table 6. Some of these are already operational.

Table 6

Area	Authority
Belfast	Northern Ireland Airports Limited
Birmingham	West Midlands Freeports Limited
Cardiff	Pearce (Wales) Consortium
Liverpool	Mersey Docks and Harbor Company
Prestwick	Kyle and Carrick District Council and British Airports Authority
Southampton	Associated British Ports

METHOD FIFTEEN: REPEALING MONOPOLIES TO LET COMPETITION GROW

A simple method of extending the reach of the private sector is to repeal the monopoly which shelters the state's domination of an activity. This alone creates an opportunity for entrepreneurs to survey the field and see where they can improve on the state's performance. Without the public monopoly to prevent their entry, they can plan to produce all kinds of new services to compete for public patronage.

When such moves are discussed in Britain, opponents raise the specter of 'cowboys' and sharp operators interested only in quick profits from easy markets, who 'skim the cream' at the top of the milk. The effect in practice, however, is to bring almost immediate improvement to the state services. Having to compete for customers encourages the public operation to seek out innovations and improvements, and to keep its prices competitive.

The public quickly benefits from the addition of the new, private services they can choose from, as well as from the improvement in services supplied by the public sector. The private companies and their employees become an industrial interest group supportive of the private sector. The power of public sector unions diminishes somewhat, as they lose the ability to completely shut down the service.

Extending the private sector by repeal of monopoly is particularly suited to public services for which consumers are charged prices. Public utilities are a good example. With the choice offered by a private alternative, the customer can decide where to put his money, and public and private suppliers will compete to help him make that decision.

Where public supply is tax-funded, however, the consumer already has his money taken for the service. Private competition here involves competing with an organization whose services are free at point of consumption, and which does not need sales to secure its funds. Obviously, there is a very limited scope for private entry into these fields.

An attractive feature of this type of privatization is that it permits the gradual change from public to private, without the need for a bruising battle to privatize the whole service. By permitting competition, it allows the public to determine the rate of privatization. It is likely that as private firms market their services and take an increasing share of the business, the public sector will be reduced accordingly. As far as the general public is concerned, they vote with their pocketbooks for the rate at which they wish the private services to expand.

This achieves a type of privatization in which the state service is not moved across to the private sector, but rather one in which an alternative supply is spawned in the private sector to take the place of a gradually shrinking public supply.

Bus and coach services

The opening up of bus and coach services on Britain's roads to much more competition from private operators gives a case history of the method of repealing public monopolies. Prices plunged and quality shot up immediately.

Moves towards the deregulation of buses and coaches in Britain had been in the air for some years. The Transport Act of 1980 relaxed the traffic licensing system in Britain. It removed licensing restrictions from new long-distance express services, excursion and tours. With the basic proviso of minimum safety regulation it became possible for anyone to run a long distance service. Moreover, the onus of proof was shifted to those who opposed the new service, and the presumption was now in favor of the applicant.

The same act also scrapped restrictions on vehicle-sharing. It allowed local authorities the right to use school buses to provide additional passenger services. It allowed local authorities to apply for 'trial area' status in which no licences (other than safety ones) would be needed.

The result of the legislation was a rapid development of express coach services and a reduction in fares on many routes. A leading state bus operator pointed out that 'with a £2 fare from London to Birmingham, it is now arguably cheaper than hitch-hiking.'

The state-run National Bus Company has remained the largest operation in the market, owing to its established network and the presence of big-city terminals, especially in London. Generally speaking, the competition to National Bus appears to be from small, localized independents, rather than from larger nationwide firms. On the London-Scotland routes the independents have 25 percent of the business based on high-quality in-coach services, with toilets, airline-quality meals, and video films.

Deregulation has had a nastier side with local authority buses sometimes deliberately using subsidies to undercut, when faced with private competition. In Cardiff, for example, the local authority buses introduced off-peak cuts in fares but only in selective areas when faced with competition from a private firm running second-hand London double-deckers on only two routes.

Further measures. As if this were not enough, a recent British government proposal outlined plans to extend the benefits of deregulation even further. At the moment only 8 percent of local bus services are run by private operators, and it is expected that a relaxation of the regulations will increase this and improve service. The government white paper introduces the idea of the shared cab, and a vehicle intermediate between the cab and the bus, as well as other proposals, including the end of road service licensing and the use of outside contractors for services which are to be subsidized.

The National Bus Company itself is to be reorganized into smaller free-standing parts which will then be transferred to the private sector. The government will welcome bids from the employees. The state agencies which regulate and provide public transport in the localities will be required to break down their operations into smaller units, which will become independent companies. Municipal bus operations will be incorporated into companies still owned by their district councils. After a suitable transition, all of these companies will stand on their own feet. They will compete with other operators for passengers and for contracts to run subsidized services.

British Telecom (BT)

The repeal of monopolies has also opened up telecommunications in Britain. The 1981 British Telecommunications Act affected British Telecom, as the national telephone system is now known, by permitting the licensing of an additional telecommunications network, Mercury, to compete with British Telecom, the licensing of private firms to provide services using the British Telecom networks, and competition in the supply of connecting equipment.

In February 1982, the Secretary of State for Industry announced the granting of a 25-year licence to Mercury, permitting it to establish and operate an independent network in competition with British Telecom. In 1990 other licences will be granted.

In the second area, other network services which compete with BT, but which use the BT network, have also been licenced, including what are called 'mail box', and 'store and forward' facilities. The Department of Industry has asked British Telecom to submit bids for new radio-telephone networks.

As for the supply of connecting equipment, it is here that the most apparent effects have been seen. Prior to the legislation the number and variety of telephones and other telecommunication apparatus was very small. A telephone in Britain until the 1980s meant the traditional black receiver with rotary dial. A recent daring innovation had introduced it in other colours. Following the legislation, there has been an enormous surge in the variety of telephones available. For the first time, there are now stores solely in the business of supplying telecommunications apparatus.

The Post Office

It was the same 1981 British Telecommunications Act which deprived British Telecom of its monopoly that also chipped away at the postal monopoly. So far the Post Office has lost its monopoly in express mail services, and private concerns are now allowed to operate centers where businesses can go to exchange documents. On top of this, registered charities are now allowed to deliver Christmas cards.

Like British Telecom, the relaxation of regulations has had a marked effect. The growth of private express parcel services in the last two years has been highly significant, with strong competition being the result.

The electricity industry

Britain's state monopoly electricity industry has seen its monopoly weakened. Since the state takeover in 1947, there had been no provision for any significant competition in the generation or the distribution of electricity. This was all changed with the passing of the 1983 Energy Bill.

Before it was permissible to sell electricity to the local areas boards only if it were produced as a surplus to one's own needs. After passage of the Bill, it became legal for a firm to be involved directly in the business of electricity generation, rather than as just a small side-line. The private firms would be allowed to use the national electricity grid for transmission to their customers, including the local area boards.

The government hopes the private involvement will act as a costing yardstick to the state sector, and thereby improve efficiency. It is also intended that the record of private innovation may bring some rewards in promoting the development of fuel sources for the future, such as wind and solar power. At the moment such innovations have not arrived and since private generation accounts for only 6 percent overall and around 15 percent of industry's supply, the development of private electricity is only in its infancy.

British Gas Corporation

Gas is yet another utility to have its monopoly breached. The 1948 Gas Act established the British gas industry under state ownership. In 1982, the Oil and Gas (Enterprise) Act, allowed the disposal of assets, and removed British Gas's monopoly as the sole buyer of North Sea gas. Private companies are now free to supply gas to users of over two million therms, using the existing pipeline network as a common carrier.

The breaking of the monopoly has caused an enormous growth of interest in the exploration and development of gas reserves. Gas exploration and appraisal wells have increased from zero between 1978 and 1980, to seventeen in 1982.

METHOD SIXTEEN: ENCOURAGING EXIT FROM STATE PROVISION

State services funded out of general taxation pose special problems. Many of them do not need to be protected by a legal monopoly since their pre-emption of funding is sufficient to give them an effective monopoly. In some cases there are already private alternatives to be found, but they are alternatives available only to those who are rich enough or prepared to sacrifice enough to use them.

Compulsory tax-funding of the state sector limits the private alternative to those who can afford to pay twice. Payment for the public sector is compulsory, whether or not it is used. To turn instead to a private supply involves rejecting the one already paid for in favor of one which must be paid for again. In such circumstances the private sector remains a luxury for the small percent of the population who can afford it. It is of little advantage to the public in general, and often finds itself on the defensive against charges of privilege and diversion of resources needed for the public service.

It might be theoretically possible to effect a sudden transformation from a tax-funded system of public supply into a system where private suppliers charge market prices, but it is not practical politics. Too many of the interest groups involved, including the general consumers, would resist such a complete step into the unknown. Consumer's fears — that the service might be eliminated altogether, or that the privately provided service would be beyond their means or inconvenient — would be reinforced by the fears of the labor force, uncertain of its own future in the private sector, and by the hostility of unions unwilling to relinquish their own hold on the public supply. In such cases privatization must be brought on slowly to be successful.

A more plausible approach is to extend gradually the facilities and services offered by private suppliers, with their prices becoming more and more attractive to potential customers. As more customers choose the private alternatives, the public service becomes progressively less able to resist the extension of those same choices and opportunities more widely across the board. The private sector will rise in importance as more and more make the decision to join it and appreciate its value. The newly satisfied consumers form an effective group in support of the private market, acting as an impediment to anyone seeking to undermine or reverse its progress.

Government can take positive steps to encourage exit from the public sector. The most useful step of all is to lower the cost of exit, making the option more widely available. Since the public sector still has to be funded, it is not possible to allow those who opt out of public supply to opt totally out of the finance of it. But it is undoubtedly possible to give some concession to those who make no more claims on the public supply. Tax rebates to those who purchase private supply is one option; allowing private payments or private insurance premiums to be tax deductible is another.

In both of these cases the state lowers the taxes required from individuals who seek private supply. The state no longer has to make provision for them, and can return part of their total tax payment accordingly. Skillfully calculated, the rebate can be at such a level that the public services that remain are progressively better funded. The return to the individuals who opt out of the public sector can be less than the savings made possible by their departure. Thus, as the public sector contracts, it can become financially better able to supply the service to those who need its services most.

Meanwhile, of course, the offering of tax concessions or rebates lowers the cost of exit. More and more people find the private supply within their price range. What started out as the prerogative of the rich gradually becomes a normal option for the bulk of the population. Extra funding is brought into the service as a whole, public and private together, and the general quality of both types of service improves.

This is one of the varieties of privatization which does not involve the transfer of resources and personnel from the public to the private sector. Instead, new and alternative resources are encouraged to develop in the private sector, and the demand for the public service gradually declines. The end result achieved is the cumulative effect of the millions of independent decisions freely taken by the population, rather than the sudden imposition upon them of a preconceived pattern.

Health insurance concessions

The granting of tax relief in Britain for some classes of private health insurance is a good example of the method of promoting private sector growth by encouraging exit from the public supply. The 1979 Conservative platform outlined the party's commitment to restoring income tax relief on employer-funded medical insurance schemes. This was done in 1981. As a result, tax relief now applies to all those earning less than £8,500 who are placed on a health scheme by their employers.

The net benefit that this has permitted is impossible to calculate accurately. The problem arises over assessment, since no records are kept, and because no direct correlation can be made between the tax relief and the number of people registering with private health firms. Nevertheless, the two main private health firms in Britain both indicate a big rise in current membership. It seems that the tax relief has been a factor in bringing the advantages of private health care to more people on lower incomes.

Social security

Britain has had a system of contracting out of social security (on and off) since 1960. In 1978, Britain launched the most comprehensive contracting-out scheme to date, with the endorsement of both the Conservative and Labor parties.

Essentially, Britain has two types of social security benefit programs. One requires manadatory participation, the other is voluntary. The first tier, the mandatory scheme, pays a benefit that is like a minimum income. All workers must pay in, and above a certain earnings level, they receive the same benefits regardless of their earnings and regardless of the amount of taxes they contributed.

The second-tier pension scheme, however, is based on earnings. The more you earn, the greater your pension. Thus, the second tier is comparable to a private pension plan. Private companies are granted the option of contracting their employees out of the second-tier benefit program and into a private pension plan. They are allowed to do so only if they provide their workers with a plan that provides benefits as good as or better than the workers would have received had they remained in the state system.

The incentive to opt out of the government's second-tier social security scheme is a tax reduction. The amount of tax reduction is chosen so that on the average, workers will find it to their financial advantage to contract out of the system. In 1983, for example, contracted-out workers received a seven percentage point payroll tax reduction. For a worker earning the average wage, this tax reduction amounted to £227.50 per year. In return for each year's tax reduction, workers forego the right to draw an annual pension of approximately £40.63.

April 1983 marked the five-year anniversary of the two-tier system, and to date it has been highly successful. Since 1978, more than forty-five percent of all British workers have contracted out of the second-tier pension scheme. Moreover, by allowing the option of contracting out, the British government has effectively cut its second-tier pension liability in half. Overall the government has reduced its entire social security liability by more than thirty percent by adopting the contracting-out system.

METHOD SEVENTEEN: USING VOUCHERS

The voucher, often proposed as a way of introducing private sector benefits and choices into education, is a specialized form of tax rebate. Rather than offering members of the public the 'free' services which tax contributions have paid for, they are offered instead a voucher which is good for the purchase of those services. The use of vouchers rather than cash is designed to ensure that the money is spent on the service, rather than 'frittered away' at the recipient's discretion.

The basic idea behind the voucher is that it gives *choice* to the consumer. Instead of receiving the usual take-it-or-leave-it service from the state, the voucher-holder can shop around before deciding where to spend it. State institutions must become consumer-responsive if they hope to get enough vouchers to finance themselves. By making the voucher also usable in the private market, and possibly by allowing consumers who are prepared to do so to spend more, an even greater range of choices is provided, including the choice of how much to spend.

Faced with the need to attract vouchers, state institutions are subject to private sector pressures. They become more cost-effective and more consumer-oriented. Innovative services are considered and produced by the private sector, with competition bringing even more beneficial effects. Thus, the voucher holds out the prospect of private sector benefits within a state system. More to the point, it promises virtual privatization without the name. Since the voucher is effectively a form of money, the state institutions which switch to voucher finance are in effect already in the private sector. The voucher holds out the prospect of immediate and dramatic inroads into universal state services.

The political record of the voucher is not good. In education the idea has been around for at least a century, and has been looked at favorably by several administrations. Despite this, it has not been given a serious trial in Britain. The reason might lie in its propensity to introduce total change. In place of the customary 'free' state service from a public institution, the voucher system allows choices in obtaining the service. Because public institutions become independently financed overnight, there is the prospect of some closing down.

Labor and management have joined forces to prevent even experimental voucher schemes, perhaps fearing a successful outcome. A dubious public has been worried by horror stories

90

which provoke an image of a new service which is all right for those with money to add, but which becomes a residual public sector rubbish dump for those without financial means. Like other privatization proposals, the voucher will be helped when it has one favorable trial to its record.

There is one form of voucher which does have a record and which is susceptible to much wider application. This is the voucher which is used to make the needy into effective bidders in a private market. The plight of the sick, the disabled, the elderly and the poor is used often to justify the imposition or maintenance of a universal state-funded service. Otherwise, it is claimed, only the well-off are able to cope. The deprived groups simply are not able to afford the service.

The obvious fallacy is that of restructuring a supply to meet a deficiency in effective demand. Clearly it is the *demand* which should be restructured. The result of the fallacy is often a public service justified only for those in need, yet governed by the drive to provide for all. All of the drawbacks of public supply are extended to the entire public because of the needs of a few.

Vouchers enter into the picture as a means of directing a subsidy to the needy themselves, rather than to the producers of the service. Vouchers are aimed at the demand instead of the supply. By giving out vouchers, the state can guarantee effective buying power to individuals who warrant support, while leaving private enterprise to provide the service. Indeed, the presence of the tokens acts as an incentive for private business to produce services catering to the voucher-holders.

One attractive feature of this scheme is that it permits a near-normal market to operate, with all of the advantages that the disciplines of the marketplace creates. At the same time, it ensures that those in special need are not left without the service. The use of tokens in this way undercuts one of the most frequent objections to the spread of private enterprise into what are deemed as essential services. By guaranteeing dependent individuals access to those services, it removes the objections, and paves the way for privatization of the service.

Transport tokens

The use of transport tokens by some British local authorities for issue to dependent groups illustrates a case history in which they can be given consumer power within the domain of private services.

In January 1973 a consortium of large governmental transport operators in Britain, including the government's transport regulatory agencies, the National Bus Company, the Scottish Bus Group and British Rail, set up National Transport Tokens. It was an attempt to form a national transport token subsidy scheme aimed at replacing the numerous local schemes which existed at that time. The system of transport tokens transfers the subsidy from the supply side to the demand side, i.e., to the transport user. In effect the tokens represent basic denominations of monetary value which can be used to buy transport services.

National Transport Tokens provides tokens in 5p, 10p, and 20p denominations. Originally there was a 2p token but it has not been sold in any quantity since 1976, and the 3p has hardly sold since 1981. Approximately 96.8 percent of all 2p tokens sold have been redeemed and the 3p token was redeemed at the 96.3 percent level. A 97.25 percent redemption rate for the higher denomination is being attempted and seems likely.

The tokens, which can be used *only* for travel on public service transport, are bought by the local authority at a discount and issued to the eligible persons. Then, after being spent on transport services within the area (including local British Rail services), they are redeemed through National Transport Tokens, which provide a modest handling premium to the operators. National Transport Tokens is, at the moment, managed by Greater Manchester Passenger Transport Executive as a non-profit organization, which means any operating surpluses are returned via discounts and premiums.

National Transport Tokens has expanded quite considerably in its ten years of operation. From a turn-over of approximately £2.3 million in 1973 and with 156 operators and 15 branches, it has grown to over a £9.3 million turn-over with 432 operators and 24 branches. By December 31, 1982, 99 authorities in the UK were using National Transport Tokens.

There have been other, more local transport token schemes, especially in the south-east of England, but they have been only moderately successful and are not on the same scale as National Transport Tokens.

METHOD EIGHTEEN: CURBING STATE POWERS

In a small number of cases, the movement towards privatization can be accelerated simply by restricting some of the state powers which oppose the movement. These may be powers exercised by particular state enterprises, or ones retained by agencies of the government. They include authority granted under previous governments with the expressed aim of increasing public sector activity at the expense of private enterprise.

A government agency with the authority to take over private business operations is an obvious candidate. If the agency is prevented from future takeovers and compelled to relinquish its current holdings, a significant withdrawal of state sector activity can ensue. In other cases it is not a direct state takeover, but encroaching state involvement which has to be dealt with by these methods.

During times of recession there is a standing temptation for politicians to attempt to 'rescue' ailing firms whose failure would bring even more unemployment. If these are in sensitive areas already hard-hit, the temptation is to make government involvement in the enterprise a prerequisite for government aid. The performance of such operations has been poor, and they invariably tempt the state into further intervention to protect its investment. In this way, the power to curb competition or to give selective advantage to state-involved enterprises grows over the years, wreaking considerable distortion by preventing the operation of an effective market.

The simple removal of these powers, or a phasing out of them, is comparatively straightforward to accomplish. The areas involved rarely affect the general public, and are more likely to have localized impact. The knowledge that the state is relinquishing its power to 'rescue' private failures is unlikely to set a specific interest group against it. Instead, there will be isolated occasions in the future when unions and workers who would have pleaded for state funds to save a company from going under will find less receptive ears.

There will be, on the other hand, competitive businesses in the private sector which stand to gain from a retreat by the state. As potential purchasers of former government assets, they represent a group which will encourage the process and keep it secure.

The method of curbing state powers can be used quite deliberately to exempt various groups from the burdens and costs of dubious regulations. The power enjoyed by agencies of the government to enforce certain types of behavior on the private sector undoubtedly raises the costs of business, contributes to the failure of existing concerns, and discourages the success of new ones.

Since compliance costs fall especially hard on small businesses, specific withdrawal of state powers can be made in their case. Powers relating to business premises, to employment and to taxation could all be curbed in the interest of promoting the easier and more rapid growth of the private sector.

Government officials

Among the case histories of curbing state powers in Britain is the reduction in powers of entry into private property, and seizure by government inspectors.

It has been accepted for a long time in Britain that the police should have the right of entry to private premises in certain circumstances. Most people, if pressed, would probably recognize that bailiffs or sheriffs ought to have certain limited powers. What is not as well known is that numerous other inspectors in the course of their duties can demand entry, keep an individual under surveillance, seize documents, seize samples of produce, inspect and copy books, accounts, and employees work-sheets. They also have a host of other powers too numerous and detailed to record.

Before 1979, no up-to-date central record existed which listed the numbers of people empowered to enter private property. Nor was there a record of the additional powers of seizure and search. In October 1979, a complete survey was published by the Adam Smith Institute. It showed that there were no less than 252 separate powers of access to private property. However, even that was claimed to be only a partial list. The Thatcher government appointed a Member of Parliament, David Mitchell, to review each department (with the exception of the

Treasury). The result was that a much larger figure emerged. For example, the Ministry for Agriculture, Fisheries and Food had rights of entry for at least 219 officials for seed and crop inspection alone.

On February 4, 1981 it was announced in *Hansard* that:

'The review of statutory powers to enter business premises which the Prime Minister announced on December 7, 1979 has now been completed by all Departments. As a result, ministers have recommended that thirty powers should be revoked and up to sixty-three modified. Most of these recommendations will be carried out in the normal course of departmental legislative programs. I am satisfied that the remaining powers are necessary, are sufficiently circumscribed and contain adequate safeguards to ensure that they do not cause unwarranted intrusion into business premises.'

For future purposes it was pointed out that arrangements were being made to scrutinize centrally all future legislation containing powers of entry to ensure they did not impose any undue burden.

METHOD NINETEEN: DIVESTMENT

Divestment means disposing by sale of state assets. In addition to passing control to the private sector by partial or total sale, or by separating off distinct entities, there are cases in which the state may sell assets which do not give it any meaningful control. When government has nationalized firms with part-holdings in other firms, or received shares of stock in return for financial subsidies, or in other ways acquired a minority holding in a private business, it has acquired new assets. These form a part of the public sector.

The state does not behave as a normal investor, and cannot be expected to. It has interests other than profitability and rates of return to think of. To some extent, a state holding is like a piece of a company removed from market influences. Consequently, the state may well find it advantageous to divest itself of these minority holdings. It might have better uses for the funds than retaining a holding in commercial activities or playing the role of investor in private markets.

Government's financial accounting can make divestment a

worthwhile operation for legislators. If the accounting system allows funds from divestment to be spent directly instead of being used to reduce the deficit, government is able to take some of the squeeze off spending without extending its red ink. The proceeds of asset sales, in other words, may be used on current spending or on new capital spending. This policy has been described by critics as 'selling the family silver to pay the butler.' If it involved only the sale of capital assets to finance excessive levels of current spending, the characterization might have merit. If, however, government takes the view that private growth has been held back by public borrowing and taxation, divestment permits it to relieve those pressures.

Divestment of minority holdings does not normally encounter entrenched opposition. Since the operations are not directly controlled by the government, opposition from the workforce is not usually a factor. There is no self-conscious class of beneficiaries who are affected by the sale. Only the few administrators who oversee government holdings in the private sector are potential adversaries to a divestment program, and they are outweighed by the potential buyers who stand to benefit from the acquisition.

British Technology Group

The British Technology Group, representing the reorganization of the National Enterprise Board and the National Research and Development Corporation, was one of the principal vehicles for government holdings in private industry.

The National Enterprise Board originally had succeeded in advancing public ownership to the healthy and profitable areas of the private sector without drawing the accusation of 'nationalizaton.' It was allowed to give aid to certain firms and to encourage the implementation of voluntary planning agreements between private concerns and the government. (The latter area was a complete failure, with only one such agreement being reached and that was with Chrysler in 1979.)

Upon its creation the National Enterprise Board was given the state's share holdings in British Leyland, Cambridge Instruments, Roll-Royce, Brown-Bovery-Kent, Herbert,

Dunford and Elliot, Ferranti, and International Computing Laboratories (ICL).

By 1978, it had acquired interests in a further 28 companies. Its power to sell off investments without the Secretary of State's permission was granted in February, 1978, provided the sale involved assets under £1 million. It was only after May, 1979, that the first moves were made toward disposing of assets, rather than acquiring them. In August 1980, new guidelines were set out by the Thatcher government obliging the NEB to sell off its profitable investments as soon as possible.

The National Enterprise Board and the National Research Development Corporation, while remaining accountable under their separate statutes, were reorganized under the banner of the British Technology Group in 1981. In 1979 it began its extensive list of asset sales (see Table 7).

In addition to these sales, the British government announced on July 12, 1984 that the company Thorn-EMI had agreed in principle to pay £95 million for the British Technology Group's shareholding in Inmos, the largest UK-owned volume manufacturer of memory and microprocessor products. Inmos has the strong prospect of a healthy future. This year its sales are expected to double again, to some £100m, giving it its first pre-tax profit, probably over £5m, since it started in 1978.

Table 7
State divestment since 1979

	Company	Receipts (£million)
1979	Hird Brown Ltd	0.40
	ICL Ltd	37.20
1980	Brown Bovery Kent (Holdings) Ltd	2.60
	Barrow Hepburn Ltd	0.27
	Computer and Systems Engineering Ltd	2.14
	Fairey Holdings Ltd	21.80
	Ferranti Ltd	55.20
	Middle East Building Services Ltd	Nominal £1 only
	New Town Securities (Northern) Ltd	0.13
	R R Chapman (Sub-Sea Surveys) Ltd	0.35
	1981 Automation and Technical Services (Holdings) Ltd	0.90

Table 7 (continued)

	Company	Receipts (£million)
	Megretti and Zambra Ltd	0.50
	System Designers International Ltd	1.19
	Energy Equipment Ltd	0.08
	CIC Investment Holdings Ltd	Nominal £1 only
	Ferranti Ltd	4.28
	1982 George P Brown Ltd	1.10
	Consine Ltd	Proceeds to arise from levy arrangements linked to sales in 1985
	Insac Products Ltd	Assets sold to Britton Lee in exchange for minority shares in that company
	Burndept Electronics Ltd	These were
	Doyce Electronics Ltd	disposed to
	F W Elliott (Holdings) Ltd	Grosvenor
	Hydraroll Ltd	Development
	Powerdrive PSR Ltd	Capital Ltd — A
	Sonicaid Ltd	private firm which
	Thandar Ltd	the NEB retains a
	Nexos Office Systems Ltd	29% holding
1983	United Medical Enterprises	15.850
(Jan-	Celltech (part disposal)	1.353
Sept)	Rigby Electronics	0.002

British Gas

British Gas reached an agreement over its 50 percent stake in Wytch Farm oilfield. A consortium referred to as the 'Dorset Five' agreed to pay a total of £215 million, in installments for the 50 percent share. The new owners — Tricentrol (with 17.5 percent), Premier Consolidated (12.5 percent), Carless Capel (7.5 percent), Clyde Petroleum (7.5 percent), and Goal Petroleum (5 percent) — will make an initial payment of £85 million, followed by a second installment when production reaches 20,000 barrels a day or a million metric tons a year. On top of this, British Gas will get a 40 percent share of the profits once production has surpassed 25 million barrels.

METHOD TWENTY: APPLYING LIQUIDATION PROCEDURES

It is conventionally assumed that the government will not allow its own enterprises to go bankrupt. Indeed, this assumption is part of the problem. The threat of bankruptcy might restrain the demands of private sector workers and their propensity to undertake industrial actions. No such compunction holds back workers in the public sector. Convinced that the enterprise cannot go broke, the battle for higher wages and better working conditions is pursued even further, with the object being to garner enough public pressure to make the government yield. If necessary, this involves pressure for a greater claim on tax revenues.

Despite the assumption that public enterprises cannot go bankrupt, there clearly are cases in which the application of bankruptcy procedures would be beneficial. The threat of winding down an industry and calling in professional liquidators to dismember it is not only a threat to restrain the demands of a powerful union. It is a valid reorganization procedure.

When liquidators are called in to pick up the debris of a private collapse, they use their skills to put as much of it as possible into packages which can be set functioning as rapidly as possible at their maximum value. The effect of their work is a repackaging of the productive elements, both capital and labor, into viable entities. Thus, the most productive and useful parts of a failed enterprise are preserved and placed elsewhere in the economy.

Parts of the public sector also may merit this treatment. It is, in essence, a speeded-up version of preparing a state enterprise with a poor record for eventual transfer. Instead of closing down the least profitable sections and streamlining production techniques in the others, a liquidation operation performs the same task abruptly in more urgent circumstances.

In a bankruptcy operation, debts are paid off in strict pro-portion to the proceeds of asset sales, and the debts are taken to be finally settled when this has been done. There clearly are public institutions to which this principle could be extended to the benefit of the general public. Instead of being a drain forever, a settlement would be made and the useful parts put to work in the competitive marketplace. As a result, there would be less dislocation of resources in the future.

Examples

Liquidation is a drastic, 'cut your losses' type of expedient reserved for cases in which it is apparent that the present organization is relatively worthless, compared to the value of having its constituents dispersed and re-allocated elsewhere. There are no 'pure' case histories in the British experience which involve the application of bankruptcy procedures to close public sector operations. There are, however, examples of closing state institutions, such as hospitals and teacher training colleges, which followed a procedure not very different. This type of treatment has been suggested for some of the poorer quality universities and colleges.

Hospitals. Considerable closures have involved hospitals. The intention was to close many of the hospitals that were un-economic, or whose work could be done at a nearby hospital. Some of the less cost-effective hospitals were closed, and their patients transferred and treated at alternative hospitals nearby. All in all, a total of twenty-seven complete hospital closures were implemented since May 1979.

Table 8
National Health Service closures since May 1979

Hospital	Date approved
NORTHERN REGION	
Overdene Maternity Home	June 1980
Willington Quay Maternity	Nov 1981
YORKSHIRE	
Headlands	Nov 1981
Townend Maternity	Aug 1979

Table 8 (continued)

Hospital	Date approved
Newton Lodge Annexe	Nov 1981
Carr Gate	Nov 1981
TRENT AREA	
Smedley Memorial	Feb 1981
Parwich	May 1981
NORTH WEST THAMES	
St Columba's	Aug 1980
Doneswood Convalescent Home	Mar 1981
Temple Hill House	Mar 1981
Leamington Park	Aug 1983
West Hendon	Sept 1983
NORTH EAST THAMES	
Bearstead Memorial	Dec 1980
Garrett Anderson Maternity Home	Sept 1979
London Jewish	Feb 1980
Prince of Wales	Nov 1983
SOUTH EAST THAMES	
St Giles	Aug 1983
SOUTH WEST THAMES	
St Benedict's	Sept 1980
South London Hospital for Women	Nov 1983
OXFORD	
Cowley Road	July 1980
SOUTH WEST	
Wendover Maternity	Aug 1983
MERSEY	
Victoria Central Hospital Surgical Unit	Jan 1981
Leasowe	Jan 1981
Cleaver	June 1983
Barrowmore	May 1982
OTHERS	
Queen Charlotte's Convalescent Home	Nov 1983

In addition, the move toward greater efficiency was continued within hospitals, as well as between them, and there were fifteen partial closures (Table 9). Particular units or wards were closed within certain hospitals, and as in the previous example, the patients are sent elsewhere.

Table 9
Partial closures, May 1979 - December 1983

Hospital	Date approved
NORTHERN	
North Tees District General	July 1981
YORKSHIRE	
Withernsea	June 1981
Stanley Royd	Nov 1981
TRENT	
Skegness and District	May 1981
EAST ANGLIA	
Bourne	Apr 1982
(Reduction in Accident and Emergency Services)	
NORTH EAST THAMES	
Royal Northern;	Apr 1982
Accident and Emergency Dept St Margarets	Apr 1982
NORTH WEST THAMES	
West Middlesex	Oct 1980
St Mary's Harrow Road	Sept 1981
West Middlesex	Oct 1981
SOUTH EAST THAMES	
Queen Mary's	Oct 1981
Preston Hall	Jan 1983
WEST MIDLANDS	
Kidderminister General	May 1982
MERSEY	
Congleton War Memorial; Maternity Unit	July 1983
Clatterbridge Accident and Emergency Dept	Jan 1981

Teacher training

Several of the state-run teacher-training colleges have been closed or amalgamated as they became unnecessary because of falling school rolls. The intention was to reduce places available on a planned schedule: 1981 — 20,200 places, 1983 — 15,200 places, 1984 — 16,300 places, and 1985 — 16,900 places.

The decision involved the ending of teacher training

completely in Huddersfield Polytechnic, North East London Polytechnic, North Staffordshire Polytechnic, Teesside Polytechnic, Thames Polytechnic, Dorset Institute of Higher Education, New College (Durham), North Cheshire College, Liverpool College of Higher Education, and De La Salle College.

In addition, certain teacher training facilities are being moved to nearby alternative institutions. This has happened in Manchester, where the College of Higher Education will give way to the polytechnic. The training at Matlock and Derby Lonsdale Colleges of Higher Education will be merged. Liverpool College of Higher Education will transfer much of its training to the polytechnic. And Leicester Polytechnic will cease to provide initial teacher training, while maintaining its postgraduate courses.

None of it, strictly speaking, is liquidation, although it does embark on a similar procedure of cutting what is unnecessary and making the remainder more cost-effective.

METHOD TWENTY-ONE: WITHDRAWAL FROM THE ACTIVITY

In a very small number of cases it is possible for government to reduce the size of the public sector by withdrawing altogether from an activity no longer deemed necessary or desirable. As the demand and need for private sector activities declines, the reduction in sales is taken as a signal to producers. Fewer and fewer remain in production, and the supply tapers off with the fall in demand.

No such effect occurs when the supply is publicly provided and financed out of general revenues. In some cases there is no real way of assessing demand at all. Output is produced with no estimate of its usefulness, or of whether the public, given a choice, would spend their money on it. What this means in practice is the survival of public services for which genuine demand has long disappeared.

It is very difficult to identify these areas. The producers, naturally enough, never acknowledge that their work is of no value. Consumers do not make decisions in such cases. One possible guide for government is the example of foreign countries. It sometimes turns out that other countries get by very well without something we have never thought of doing without.

For areas of public supply which involve a product or service, there are crude measures of demand. A state bus service which has carried only one person a day for the last ten years is clearly unnecessary, since it can be withdrawn, and some other transportation subsidy provided to the riders if necessary. But in fields such as regulation, the public demand for an activity is not expressed even through the political process. In some cases not even government knows exactly what services continue to be produced long after any need for them has departed.

By mounting a campaign to identify and eliminate public services which no longer are needed, government will undoubtedly antagonize the bureaucracy whose jobs are threatened. This is the sort of campaign which the media, on the other hand, can be enlisted to support. They tend to enjoy exposing misuse of public funds and taking a stance as public watchdogs. Thus there may be small areas of unnecessary public sector activity where the balance of interests permits government to withdraw altogether.

Public bodies

The government elected in Britain in 1979 embarked on a systematic and sustained campaign to identify and eliminate some of the para-governmental 'quango' bureaucracy. The abolition of hundreds of these bodies provides some instances of a total withdrawal from activities. The key factor which makes this process possible is that a service which is no longer necessary finds little interest group support to sustain it. What is required, however, is a very public campaign to highlight the useless and expensive nature of such activities.

The quango, more formally known as the Quasi-Autonomous National Governmental Organization, is a prime example of the slow but sure growth of government in recent times. Attempts to curb and even dispose of quangos were bedeviled by the most basic of problems: lack of knowledge. The best working definition was put forward by Sir Philip Holland in his book, *The Governance of Quangos*, published by the Adam Smith Institute, who said that 'a quango is an official body to which a minister makes appointments other than civil servants.'

The problems with quangos and rule by quangos are sixfold. First, there is the shift of power away from the control and scrutiny of Parliament. Second, quangos provide excessive patronage for politicians. Third, they have been used as a means of by-passing Parliament, and of allowing party political objectives to be achieved without the prolonged debate which accompanies the legislative process. Fourth, quangos crowd out private effort. Fifth, they can constitute taxation without representation. Quangos such as the Industrial Training Boards levy a tax on companies which carry the burden of quango decisions, yet they are not elected. Finally, quangos represent the decline of democracy. Decision making is being passed away from the legislature and toward the bureaucrats. Similar effects are visible in the operation of some of America's regulatory agencies.

It was not until 1979 that extensive research work by the Adam Smith Institute gave the first real glimpse at the numbers involved. A total of 3,068 individual bodies, representing 947 different types of quangos, were identified, with the total fees and salaries paid to the main category of 838 quangos amounting to £3,320,000, plus expenses in 1977-78. Other figures indicating large expenses amounting to millions of pounds for other quangos resulted in governmental action.

At the end of August 1979, a civil servant, Sir Leo Pliatzky, was appointed by Mrs Thatcher to undertake a full review. In January 1980, a government white paper on *Non-Departmental Public Bodies* listed 2,117 quangos, although it excluded the Nationalized Industry Boards, the National Health Service, the Broadcasting Authorities, to name but a few. It is worth comparing these figures with the calculations of Sir Philip Holland MP:

'At the time of the general election of May 1979, my own researches revealed that there were 3,068 quangos in Britain, involving 40,000 quangurus (appointees sitting on quangos), 10,000 of whom were in receipt of salaries to the total value of approximately £8 million.'

In the press following the announcement, it was suggested that of the 2,117 organizations examined 246 should disappear, and that 3,700 ministerial appointments and 250 permanent posts should be terminated, achieving a total saving of £11.6

million. By the end of the year the government had improved on that expectation. It announced the demise of 290 of the report's quangos, and a reduction in the number of quangurus by nearly 4,000. Furthermore, reduction in the planned programs of the larger quangos such as the National Enterprise Board, the British National Oil Corporation and the Manpower Services Commission meant further savings of £350 million during 1980-81.

In December 1980, the government announced anticipated savings of nearly £23 million by the abolition of 436 quangos by 1983. The Prime Minister had said that the decision in January to abolish 246 bodies saving £11.6 million had been supplemented by the winding up of another 28 executive bodies and 164 advisory and judicial bodies.

Since then there has been a decline in anti-quango fervor, but interest is still strong. Using the government's definition, a more recent appraisal of the success in quango-culling was given by the Prime Minister in January 1982, when in reply to a written question she stated that 441 non-departmental public bodies had already been abolished or reduced, and 109 more were scheduled for abolition or reduction by April 1984.

METHOD TWENTY-TWO: THE RIGHT TO PRIVATE SUBSTITUTION

There are areas of the public sector for which the general public could be given the right to select private alternatives. Given the characteristics of public monopoly, there are several state services about which the public frequently complains of delays in service and quality of work. By giving the public the right to turn to private businesses for the same products, and to bill the state for the cost of the job, competition is given a major foothold.

Obviously, if government is footing the bills, it has to have a degree of control over costs. The price limit it can accept will bear close relation to what the job would have cost had it been undertaken by the public sector. This is a practical problem which can be solved by recourse to some independent body such as an auditor. Broadly speaking, for the policy to succeed, there must be a readily available method of determining in advance the price government can reasonably be expected to pay for public services performed by a private company.

106

Once the practical problem is solved, a range of opportunities presents itself. In Britain, repairs and maintenance of public housing, roads, utilities and other public infrastructures are all potential candidates for this treatment. If the citizens concerned obtain estimates from private sector companies which are within the acceptable cost limits, they can call in the contractors to get the job done.

The public at large gains visibly if this policy is adopted. As a large interest group, they perceive its benefit and can be counted on to support the extension of choice and opportunity for faster and better services. Private businesses form another interest group on the plus side, as they see the profit potential for themselves.

The managers and workers who provide the public service are on the negative side, but the effect on them is a gradual one. With more frequent use of private alternatives, the need for a large public establishment diminishes. The public operation will shrink gradually as the demand shifts, with displaced employees being taken up in many cases by growing private companies.

The implementation of a right to substitute private supply is one of the newer weapons in the arsenal of privatization. It is also one of the most promising in that it increases the choice available to the general public. Opposition to it has to be based on the claim that there should be no such opportunity for choice, and that people should be forced to depend only on the public sector and on the quality and speed of service which it produces. This is a weak position politically, with most interest groups heavily on the side of extending choice.

Water and housing

During an industrial dispute involving the water authorities in Britain, the recently-retired Master of the Rolls, Lord Denning, expressed the opinion that householders had the right in law to bring in private contractors to repair damaged water pipes, and to bill the water authority for the work. Although the dispute ended before anyone could launch a test case, this illustrates the substitution method of privatization.

Measures to allow tenants of public housing in Britain a 'right to repair' and to bill the local government provides a case history of private substitution. The Housing and Building Control Act of 1984 is concerned with tenants rights and the disposal of state-owned houses. Under Section 28, it amends the 1980 Housing Act to allow the Secretary of State to introduce by regulation a scheme to allow public housing tenants a right to carry out their own repairs and to obtain reimbursement from their landlords for doing so. This right to repair will allow a tenant to recoup a percentage of the costs from the local authority.

In theory, the idea has great potential. One would expect an increase in the general level of repairs to publicly-owned houses, and—perhaps in the long run— a decline in the average cost per house for repairs because they would be performed privately, and at lower cost. Ultimately, the technique offers a new form of choice to break the state monopoly. It would be very effective in the event of a withdrawal of the state service during an industrial dispute.

6. FUTURE PRIVATIZATION IN BRITAIN

British Steel Corporation

On December 21, 1983, a new company, United Ring, was started. British Steel and two private sector companies, Woodhouse and Rixcon (Holdings), and Inco Alloy Products, announced on that date that they were intending to merge their ring-rolled products businesses. Larzard Brothers, the merchant bank which put the proposals together, will receive 12.5 percent of United Ring shares, while British Steel will take 25 percent of the shares in the company valued at £10.5 million with a turnover of around £30 million. The remainder of the shares will be split equally between the two private firms who will pay £910,000 each. It is unlikely, however, that the firm will be fully privatized for some time.

British Airways

Hopes are high for the sale of a portion of the shares in British Airways in the spring of 1985. This will be four years since the passing of the Civil Aviation Act of 1980 which changed its status from a public corporation into a limited liability company with the Trade Secretary holding the shares.

The delay in privatization has been attributed to the financial problems which began with BA's enormous losses in 1980. The final decision on the timing of privatization had to depend on the airline's financial performance, on the state of the stock-market and on the general prospects for the airline industry. However, BA made a net profit in the 1983-84 financial year of £181 million.

Other prospects

(1) British Gas Corporation. Consideration is being given to the idea of selling off the corporation's 500 showrooms and a positive decision is expected soon. There are expectations also that BGC's gas interests will be separated off and then sold.

(2) Heavy goods vehicle testing stations. Negotiations are proceeding between the Secretary of State for Transport and Lloyd's Register of Shipping. A transfer to Lloyd's Testing Ltd is imminent.

(3) Royal ordnance factories. Considerable investigation and debate have delayed the privatization of the Royal Ordnance (Ammunition) Factories. Nevertheless, it was decided in 1984 that a public limited company will be registered as Royal Ordnance plc and will become the sole owner of four limited companies — Royal Ordnance Ammunition Limited, Royal Ordnance Explosives Limited, Royal Ordnance Small Arms Limited, and Royal Ordnance Weapons and Fighting Vehicles Limited.

(4) Cable broadcasting. The vast majority of investment in cable broadcasting will be from the private sector — despite a general assumption by opposition political parties that the state should be heavily involved.

(5) British Waterways Board. The British Waterways Board will make attempts to increase opportunities for the private sector by direct investment, contracting out, joint ventures and selling off separate sections.

(6) British Telecom. Following the successful sale of British Telecom, the government is under pressure to sell more of its 49% holding.

(7) British Leyland. Before the end of the current term of office, the government hopes to sell some of British Leyland's subsidiaries including Rolls Royce, Land-Rover and Uni-part, its components division.

(8) British Shipbuilders. British Shipbuilders' warshipbuilding interests are to be privatized by March 1986. In the meantime the corporation has also been instructed to continue to dispose of its other sizeable assets.

(9) Inland Revenue sorting offices. The use of private contractors to take on work for the Inland Revenue (Britain's IRS) has been proposed.

(10) British Airports Authority. Privatization is being considered, but the method is not yet agreed upon. It appears that four out of the seven airports the authority owns are making a loss even if BAA as a whole is profitable. Legislation is unlikely before late 1985.

(11) Gibraltar dockyard. The Royal Naval Dockyard in Gibraltar closed on December 31, 1984, but re-opened immediately as the Gibraltar Ship Repair Company a commercially managed enterprise of A & P Appledore International Ltd.

(12) Electricity Generating Board. The Central Electricity Generating Board held negotiations with the company Taylor Woodrow, whose subsidiary, Taylor Woodrow Energy, is interested in buying a 180-megawatt oil-fired power station in the center of Plymouth. Interest has also been expressed in the coal-fired Carmarthen Bay station and the Rogerstone power station in South Wales. Other projects may well be discussed in the future.

(13) British Rail. British Rail has been directed by the government to put forward proposals for more private sector finance and participation in the development of railway services.

(14) The National Film and Television School. The government has reached an agreement with the cinemas, the independent television companies, and the BBC to fund the National Film and Television School to the level of £600,000 a year. This will replace the funding from the Eady Levy (a tax on cinema receipts) used solely to fund the NFTS and other film projects.

(15) The National Film Finance Corporation. As well as having made arrangements with certain organizations in the film, television, and video sectors to provide private funding for the future, the National Film Finance Corporation is to be formed into a new company in the near future.

(16) National Health Service housing. The recent Rayner Scrutiny Report on National Health Service residential accommodation showed that up to £750 million could be released instantly by the sale of surplus NHS property. A suggestion the British government appears attracted to involves selling the property to sitting tenants — similar to the way in which council house sales have proceeded.

(17) Crown Agents. Proposals for the reorganization of the Board of Crown Agents, who manage state property overseas, had been broadly accepted by the government with a view to their privatization. It is expected that this may occur in 1986.

(18) Britoil. An offering of some, if not most, of the government's remaining shareholding in Britoil has been suggested, especially in the light of its better-than-expected profit announcement in March 1984.

(19) Short Brothers. Short Brothers airplane factory based in Northern Ireland is due for privatization.

(20) British Steel Corporation. Although it has been government policy since 1979 to seek the transfer of British Steel's assets and activities to the private sector, only a little has been achieved in this respect. Nevertheless, serious discussions continue.

(21) British Aerospace. The British government no longer considers sacrosanct the 25 percent minimum shareholding it said it would retain in British Aerospace. At present it still possesses 48.4 percent of the issued shares in BAe, and appears willing to reduce that.

7. CONCLUSION

From the variety of techniques of privatization, and from the case histories of progress made under each, it is obvious that privatization is a complex and subtle process.

It is not a panacea or a formula. Instead it is an approach which can generate and focus creative policy ideas. Overwhelmingly, the impression emerges that each case is unique and requires a different remedy. Even so simple an objective as selling a public corporation on the stock market can be accomplished by many possible methods. Several of these have been put into practice.

Politicians in the United States and Britain are not short of critics telling them to cut public spending. What they are short of is people telling them how to do it with advantage. No American president is going to abolish Social Security, any more than a British prime minister is going to abolish the National Health Service. The attempt to do either would be politically suicidal and it would fail.

If choice and opportunity are to be introduced into these two systems so that innovative alternatives will be offered to consumers (and so that preferences can be satisfied and the burden of public spending be reduced), creative policies will be needed to give people the opportunity to turn to private equivalents. By such means it is possible to build up private sector supply through the exercise of the free choices of individuals, without threatening the generally perceived benefits of the public supply.

All too often the critics of public spending behave like a poor ski instructor, pushing a reluctant government down the slopes toward the goal of a reduced public sector at the bottom. Of course, with such a clumsy, direct approach the hapless legislors come to grief on the first interest group and end up in a shower of broken limbs and skis. More thoughtful preparation would have devised a slalom course, steering the skier around the interest groups and down a safer path which enables the objective to be achieved.

It is in this spirit that the creative work on privatization has to be performed. Each part of the public sector requires a different path; each part has different interest groups entrenched along the way. The best that can be hoped for is that each can be dealt with one by one, and that the skier's skill and confidence will improve with each success.

There is a further impression created by the experience of privatization in Britain. It is that large though the progress has been, and successful though the techniques have proved, the process is still in its very early stages. As attention moves from the industries to the utilities, and from there to state services and regulatory functions, the sheer size of the task ahead is staggering.

On the other hand, there are hopeful signs. Those addicted to folk wisdom might note that a good beginning is halfway through, and the first half is always the hardest. It might be difficult to set the boulder rolling downhill, but it certainly becomes easier after that. The very success of what has been done already is the biggest factor contributing to further success. Delighted and reassured by the results of what already has been done, people are ready for more. Meanwhile, the opponents grow weaker as their predictions of calamity are disproved time after time. The process may be only beginning, but it is gathering speed and momentum.

All of this should give heart to policy analysts in the United States. However large it was in Britain, the public sector is in retreat. A similar achievement could take place in America.

Certainly, solutions in the US will be different. The American political and judicial systems will necessitate home-grown policies tailored to US institutions. But if the questions and the answers are different, the determination can be the same.

There is no shortage of Americans committed to freedom and determined to win back for individuals some of the choices taken from them by the state. There is no lack of will and creativity either, as witnessed by the continued vitality of the private economy despite all of the burdens imposed upon it. Privatization offers a process which can turn entrepreneurial talent to work on the political system, bringing creative inputs to bear on public problems. If the public sector is big, then so are the opportunities it offers to diminish it. If it is daunting, then so much more challenge it offers to the creative and adventurous temperament. The state can be conquered by human care and effort.